Materials for the Islamic History of Semipalatinsk: Two Manuscripts by Aḥmad-Walī al-Qazānī and Qurbānᶜalī Khālidī

edited by:

Allen J. Frank and Mirkasyim A. Usmanov

Contents

Introduction: Semipalatinsk and the Islamic History of Imperial Russia 1

Aḥmad-Walī al-Qazānī (1833-1901) 9

The History book of the City of Semipalatinsk (English Translation) 12

Kitāb-i Tawārīkh-i Sīmī Pūlāṭ Qalʿa (Facsimile) 38

Qurbānʿalī Khālidī (1846-1913) 63

History of Semipalatinsk by Qurbānʿalī Khālidī (English Translation) 68

History of Semipalatinsk by Qurbānʿalī Khālidī (Turkic Text) 83

Introduction: Semipalatinsk and the Islamic History of Imperial Russia*

Semipalatinsk was one of the largest and most influential of imperial Russia's Islamic religious and educational centers, rivaled only by the better documented centers of Kazan and Orenburg. Containing one of the largest concentrations of wealthy Muslim merchants and Muslim merchant capital in Russia, the city at its peak supported no less than eleven mosques and more significantly, nine permanently staffed and functioning *madrasas*.[1] The Sufis and scholars of Semipalatinsk were part of an Islamic network linked primarily to the Volga-Ural region, Central Asia (especially to Bukhara, but also to Samarqand, Tashkent, and the Ferghana Valley), Chinese Turkestan, Turkey, and Egypt. The *madrasas* of Semipalatinsk attracted students from throughout the eastern Kazakh steppe, and supplied scholars to communities throughout eastern Kazakhstan, including communities in Chinese Turkestan.

Despite its stature as one of Russia's premier Muslim centers, Semipalatinsk is also the most poorly documented, at least in published sources. A major reason for the almost complete absence of Semipalatinsk and its Sufis and scholars in the biographical literature is certainly its tremendous distance from Kazan and Orenburg, the centers of Islamic culture in the Volga-Ural region, being roughly 2,600 kilometers from Kazan. However, Semipalatinsk differed in a number of important ways from the other major Muslim cultural centers located along the Kazakh steppe, such as Astrakhan, Ural'sk,

---

* The authors wish to thank Michael Kemper and Juergen Paul for their editorial help in preparing this paper.

1 *Madrasas* were without question the most prestigious of Muslim religious institutions in imperial Russia. The concentration of *madrasas* in rural areas tended to be relatively low, even in areas of dense Muslim settlement. While every mosque typically supported a *maktab*, districts with thirty or forty mosques typically supported only a handful of *madrasas*, if any. In cities *madrasas* tended to be more commonly and permanently established. In this respect Semipalatinsk, with its nine permanently functioning *madrasas*, must be viewed as being on par with the largest Muslim centers of imperial Russia, including Kazan, Orenburg, and Astrakhan; cf. Allen J. Frank, *Muslim Religious Institutions in Imperial Russia: the Islamic World of Novouzensk District and the Kazakh Inner Horde, 1780-1910*, (Leiden, 2001), 232-255.

Orenburg, Troitsk, and Petropavlovsk. In these cities, as well as in Kazan, Muslims were usually minorities, living in separate settlements, either near the centers of the cities, as in Kazan and Astrakhan, or in separate towns some distance from the cities, such as Qarghalï, near Orenburg, or Mamliutka near Petropavlovsk. By contrast, Semipalatinsk can be considered the only *Muslim* major city in Russia proper, with Muslims forming an absolute majority of the population probably already by the beginning of the nineteenth century;[2] in the second half of the nineteenth century numerous travelers commented on the city's overall "oriental appearance,"[3] which they felt distinguished it from the other cities along the Kazakh steppe they had visited. Furthermore, unlike in other cities, where Tatars dominated the urban Muslim population, in Semipalatinsk the largest single Muslim ethnic group in the city were Kazakhs, who outnumbered the Tatar and Central Asian communities combined and made up the majority of students in Semipalatinsk's *madrasas*.

Another possible reason for Semipalatinsk's neglect in published sources is that it appears to have been a bastion of traditionalism, despite a mounting tide of Islamic modernism that gained strength in Russia in the first two decades of the twentieth century. Qurbānᶜalī Khālidī tells us in his manuscript that Islamic modernism, or jadidism, came very late to the *madrasas* of Semipalatinsk, only after 1907, and that by 1912 educators had deemed the jadidist curriculum unsuitable for children, when it was dropped in favor of more traditional methods.[4] Unlike nearly every other major Muslim

---

2 According to N. Abramov, by the 1850's Muslim made up 41 percent of the city's population; cf. · Nikolai Abramov, "Oblastnyi gorod Semipalatinsk," *Zapiski Imperatorskago russkago geograficheskago obshchestva*, vol. 1/1, 1861, section 2, 141. However, his numbers appear to exclude the city's Tatar population, and it is likely that already by the beginning of the nineteenth century Muslims formed a majority of the city's population. In any case, by 1882 Muslims made up 62 percent of the city's population; cf. Zhanuzak Kasymbaev, *Istoriia goroda Semipalatinska* (1718-1917 gg.), (Almaty, 1998), 95.

3 Cf. V. V. Radlov, *Iz Sibiri*, (Moscow, 1989), 73; Abramov, "Oblastnyi gorod Semipalatinsk," 123; George Kennan, *Siberia and the Exile System* I, (London, 1891), 157.

4 The rejection of jadidist education in Semipalatinsk's *madrasas* by 1912 suggests a need to reevaluate how dominant the jadidist curriculum actually

center in Russia, Semipalatinsk did not publish a single Tatar journal or newspaper before 1917. By contrast, Tatars in Kazan, Orenburg, Astrakhan and other towns were publishing dozens of journals and newspapers.[5] The conservatism of Semipalatinsk's Muslim community is alluded to in a variety of sources. A Russian observer noted in the 1860's that Tatar women generally walked about the city with their heads completely covered, save for one eye, a custom that was much less common in the Volga-Ural region.[6] At the end of his manuscript Aḥmad-Walī notes proudly that European affectations and habits are all but absent among the city's Muslims. The reasons and even the nature of Semipalatinsk's traditionalism and conservatism cannot be determined without a detailed evaluation of the city's Islamic discourse, a portion of which has come down to us. However, its traditionalism cannot be simply explained by the city's close ties with Central Asia, since the major jadid centers of the Volga-Ural region, such as Orenburg, Ural'sk and Kazan enjoyed equal, if not deeper, connections with Bukhara and other Central Asian cities. A possible explanation may be found in the city's large Kazakh population. We can simply dismiss as ill-informed the all too commonly encountered cliché that Tatar merchants converted the Kazakhs to Islam in the nineteenth century and that these Kazakhs were "lightly" Islamized, and consequently were unorthodox or essentially "shamanistic." This view is usually encountered in the works of Kazakh nationalists, Soviet scholars, and Western modernists, who as often as not seem to be expressing their own wishful thinking on the subject.

---

was at that time. Elsewhere, evidence from Novouzensk district, in Samara Province on the western edge of the Kazakh steppe, suggests that in rural areas Muslims greeted jadidism for the most part with apathy, and most of the jadidist schools that opened in Novouzensk district were soon forced to close because of a lack of students; cf. Frank, *Muslim Religious Institutions*, 246-250.

5 In the most complete survey to date of the Tatar press in Imperial Russia, Dilyara Usmanova only identifies two Muslim newspapers that were published in Semipalatinsk, *Khalq sūzī* and *Ḥurrīyat dūlqinlarī*, both of which only began publication following the February Revolution in 1917; cf. Dilyara M. Usmanova, "Die tatarische Presse 1905-1918: Quellen, Entwicklungsetappen und quantitative Analyse," *Muslim Culture in Russia and Central Asia* [vol.1], Michael Kemper, Anke von Kügelgen, Dmitriy Yermakov eds., (Berlin, 1996), 265.

6 Abramov, "Oblastnyi gorod Semipalatinsk," 143.

Rather, the evidence from a variety of local Muslim sources suggests the opposite, that in fact the Kazakhs, while perhaps on the whole poorly educated, were intensely orthodox in their practice, and in fact provided examples of piety and orthopraxis to their Tatar and Sart neighbors.[7]

The two manuscripts which are being published in this study are major and heretofore unknown sources for Islamic culture in imperial Russia in general, and for the city of Semipalatinsk in particular. They are primarily histories of Semipalatinsk's Muslim religious institutions: the city's mosques, *madrasas* and *ᶜulamā*, as well as the merchants who supported these institutions. The manuscripts provide us with unparalleled and detailed information on the personalities which constituted this major Islamic cultural center and also provide us with unique evidence on the scholarly and Sufi networks that linked Semipalatinsk and eastern Kazakhstan with the rest of the Islamic world.

The Emergence of a Muslim City on the Russian Steppe Frontier

The two manuscripts provide mainly accurate, if very general, information on the growth of Semipalatinsk in the eighteenth century. To be more precise, we can add that Semipalatinsk was founded in 1718 as a fortified post on the Irtysh line. The original settlement was built on a site subsequently known as Staraia Krepost'; in 1776 it was moved to its present location several kilometers away. While Qurbānᶜalī and Aḥmad-Walī offer their own accounts of the origin of the name Semipalatinsk, Russian sources from the eighteenth century relate that the name derives from the

7 In addition to Aḥmad-Walī al-Qazānī's evaluation of Kazakh piety, cf. Jahānshāh b. ᶜAbdaljabbār an-Nīzhghārūṭī, *Tārīkh-i Astarkhān*, (Astrakhan, 1907), 25-28; Allen J. Frank "Islam and Ethnic Relations in the Kazakh Inner Horde: Muslim Cossacks, Tatar Merchants and Kazakh Nomads in a Turkic Manuscript, 1870-1910," *Muslim Culture in Russia and Central Asia from the 18th to the Early 20th Centuries*. Vol. 2, 233-235; Qurbānᶜalī Khālidī discusses Kazakh orthodoxy and piety in detail in his major published work; cf. Qurbānᶜalī Khālidī, *Tawārīkh-i khamsa-yi sharqī*, (Kazan, 1910), 453 and passim.

presence of seven Buddhist monasteries at the site (*sem' palatok*).[8] Although the development of Semipalatinsk as a mainly Muslim city only took place in the nineteenth century, it appears that Muslims had always been present in the city; initially Bashkir Cossacks were settled in the city for garrison duty on a rotating basis, and by 1754 we know that the city had a merchant quarter inhabited by Russian and Central Asian merchants.[9] By the end of the eighteenth century the city had 550 residents, and as our manuscripts inform us, there were at least two *maḥallas*, one for Central Asians, and one for Tatars (or "Nughays" as they called themselves). Captain Ivan Andreev, a Russian officer who was based in Semipalatinsk in the 1770's and 1780's, wrote that in 1785 one hundred Bashkirs were garrisoned in Semipalatinsk, together with fifty Tobol'sk and Tiumen' "Service Tatars."[10] He also remarked on the presence of a substantial Tatar merchant population at that time.

Muslim immigration to the city continued throughout the first half of the nineteenth century. Central Asian merchants settled in large numbers in the 1820's and 1830's.[11] At this time even larger numbers of Kazakhs began settling permanently in the city. These were for the most part pauperized families too poor to own their own livestock, and forced to work as laborers in the city. These Kazakhs, called *yataqs* or *zhataqs*, mainly lived in a suburb of the city south of the Irtysh called the Zarechnaya Sloboda.[12] In the 1850's the city had three large sections. North of the Irtysh River, the northern part of the city was called the Cossack Quarter (Kazatskaia Sloboda) and was reportedly the most prosperous section of the city. To the

---

8 On these structures cf. Abramov, "Oblastnyi gorod Semipalatinsk," 116-119; A. D. Kolesnikov (ed.), *Opisanie Tobol'skogo namestnichestva*, (Novosibirsk, 1982), 316; I. A. Kastan'e, *Drevnosti Kirgizskoi stepi i Orenburgskago kraia* (Trudy Orenburgskoi uchenoi arkhivnoi komissii XXII), (Orenburg, 1910), 141-143.

9 Kasymbaev, *Istoriia goroda Semipalatinska*, 52, 54.

10 I. G. Andreev, *Opisanie Srednei ordy kirgiz-kaisakov*, (Almaty, 1998), 146; Muslim Cossacks were withdrawn from the Irtysh Line in 1809, after which the line was manned by permanent settlements of the Siberian Cossack Host.

11 Kasymbaev, *Istoriia goroda Semipalatinska*, 92.

12 Kasymbaev, *Istoriia goroda Semipalatinska*, 92-93, 96.

south was the Tatar Quarter (Tatarskaia Sloboda), which made up the largest part of the city and was inhabited by various Muslim groups. Russian observers at that time noted that this part of the city differed architecturally from the Russian section. In the Tatar Quarter houses tended to be built in the Central Asian style, in which windows looked out into an inner courtyard, rather than into the street.[13] South of the Irtysh was the large suburb known as the Zarechnaia Sloboda. This was the poorest section of the city, inhabited primarily by Kazakhs as well as by some Tatars. This part of the city was composed of two separate suburbs. The one directly across from the city was called Semipalatinskaia and the one further up the river was called Dzhulamanka.[14]

In 1882 Russians made up only 35.5 percent of the city's population, while Kazakhs made up 36.6, Tatars 22.9, and Sarts 2.9 (by contrast, Muslims made up less than two percent of the population in Omsk). Another tally, which probably excluded the heavily Kazakh Zarechnaia Sloboda, is as follows:

Russians	7,342
Kazakhs	6,647
Tatars	3,642
Sarts	509
Bashkirs	31
Others	176 [15]

Another significant demographic fact is that not only did Kazakhs form the largest single group in the city, but Semipalatinsk had one of the largest concentrations of sedentary Kazakhs in the Russian empire. While most Kazakhs were pauperized, working as laborers and small craftsmen, there were some wealthy merchants among them, including Tinūbāy Kōkān ōghlī, a merchant of the Third Guild, and others whom Qurbānᶜalī and Aḥmad-Walī identify as having built mosques.[16] Despite the poverty of the Kazakhs in

---

13 Kasymbaev, *Istoriia goroda Semipalatinska*, 83.
14 Abramov, "Oblastnyi gorod Semipalatinsk," 121.
15 Kasymbaev, *Istoriia goroda Semipalatinska*, 95.
16 Kasymbaev, *Istoriia goroda Semipalatinska*, 96-97.

the city, it is evident that they played a major role in the city's Muslim educational institutions. Already in the 1830's, out of 194 students studying "in mosques," 90, or close to half, were Kazakhs (96 were Tatars and 8 were Central Asians)[17] and Aḥmad-Walī remarks that Kazakhs made up the majority of the city's *shāgirds* by 1888.

Central Asian merchants constituted the smallest community among Semipalatinsk's Muslims. Until the Russian conquest of Central Asia in the 1860's, these merchants lived in Semipalatinsk mainly as foreign subjects. The community, composed of subjects of the khanate of Qoqand, was headed by an headman, called an *āqsaqāl*. According to Qurbānᶜalī the *āqsaqāl* was appointed by the khan of Qoqand, and the first *āqsaqāl* in Semipalatinsk was Mīrqurbān Bāy b. Mu'min, known in Russian sources as the *starshina* Mirkurban Niiazov.[18] The Central Asian merchants came primarily from Tashkent and the Ferghana Valley, and were probably already settled in Semipalatinsk in the first half of the eighteenth century. The local Central Asians were known as Chala Kazakhs, descendants of Central Asian or Tatar fathers and Kazakh mothers. Early on the Chala Kazakhs dominated the Kazakh trade, and also the Central Asian caravan trade to a degree.[19] Semipalatinsk was one of the major hubs of the caravan trade linking Russia with Central Asia, Chinese Turkestan, Mongolia and Tibet. Semipalatinsk, with its customs post, was the main port of entry into Russia for merchants from Tashkent, the Ferghana Valley, and Chinese Turkestan who were headed to markets in Russia proper, especially Kazan, Irbit, Nizhnii Novgorod, and Moscow.[20]

As a permanent community in the city the position of the Central Asians appears to have eroded substantially after the

---

17 Kasymbaev, *Istoriia goroda Semipalatinska*, 143.

18 On this institution in Russia and in Chinese Turkestan cf. Qurbānᶜalī Khālidī, *Tawārīkh-i khamsa-yi sharqī*, 366-367.

19 On the Chala Kazakhs cf. Qurbānᶜalī Khālidī, *Tawārīkh-i khamsa-yi sharqī*, 384-391.

20 Kasymbaev, *Istoriia goroda Semipalatinska*, 111-112, 115; for more details on Central Asian trade with Semipalatinsk cf. Kh. Z. Ziiaev, *Ekonomicheskie sviazi Srednei Azii s Sibir'iu v XVI-XIX vv.*, (Tashkent, 1983).

Russian conquest of Tashkent and the Ferghana Valley. Nikolai Abramov notes that in the 1850's there were over 1,000 Central Asians resident in the city, but by 1882 their number had fallen to 509.[21] Aḥmad-Walī alludes to the moral and economic degeneration he felt they were experiencing by 1888. Nevertheless Qurbānᶜalī describes how a wealthy Central Asian was still able to renovate one of their mosques in 1911. In any case, the Central Asians appear to have played a much smaller role in the city's religious life than the Tatars or Kazakhs. The Central Asians' two mosques, called Sart or Chala Kazakh mosques, did not support *madrasas*, whereas the nine Tatar and Kazakh mosques all supported *madrasas*.

The third major Muslim group in Semipalatinsk were Tatars, who referred to themselves by the ethnonym "Nughay."[22] Tatar and Bashkir Cossacks, interpreters, and merchants played a major role in facilitating Russian expansion into the Kazakh steppe; of particular importance were Tatar religious figures, who played a crucial role in steppe diplomacy from the 1730's through to the end of the nineteenth century.[23] While outnumbered by Kazakhs, Tatars were clearly the dominant Muslim group in the city. Tatar merchants gradually came to dominate the caravan trade, manufacturing, and the retail trade, especially after the Russian conquest of the Central Asian khanates. Tatar merchants, as elsewhere on the Kazakh steppe, enjoyed close relations with the Russian authorities, playing

---

21 Abramov, "Oblastnyi gorod Semipalatinsk," 140; Kasymbaev, *Istoriia goroda Semipalatinska*, 95.

22 The name "Nughay" was widely used by Kazakhs and Central Asians to refer to Volga Tatars and the term came to be adopted as a self-appelation among Tatars residing in close proximity to the Kazakh steppe; cf. Frank "Islam and Ethnic Relations," 216-217; Jahānshāh an-Nīzhghārūṭī, *Tārīkh-i Astarkhān*, 25-28. Among Tatars in eastern Kazakhstan a number of legends even circulated, connected to the Bulghar conversion cycle, in which the name "Nughay" was said to have been given to the Tatars' ancestors by the Prophet Muhammad himself via three of his Companions (*ṣaḥābas*); cf. Qurbānᶜalī Khālidī, *Tawārīkh-i khamsa-yi sharqī*, 176-180; on the Bulghar conversion legends of the Volga-Ural region cf. Allen J. Frank, *Islamic Historiography and Bulghar Identity among the Tatars and Bashkirs of Russia*, (Leiden, 1998), passim.

23 Cf. Allen Frank, "Tatarskie mully sredi kazakhov i kirgizov v XVIII-XIX vekakh" *Kul'tura, iskusstvo tatarskogo naroda: istoki, traditsii, vzaimosviazi* (Kazan, 1993) 124-131; A. Zeki Velidi Togan, *Bügünkü Türkili (Türkistan) ve Yakın Tarihi*, (Istanbul, 1981), 325-332.

major roles as intermediaries with the Kazakh nomads. The more humble stratum of the Tatar community was made up of craftsman, artisans, and petty traders who were generally more prosperous than their largely pauperized Kazakh co-religionists. However, it was in the realm of religious institutions that we can say that Tatars were dominant. Tatars not only dominated Semipalatinsk's "official" religious institutions, but they also dominated those of eastern Kazakhstan as a whole, including the towns of Ust'-Kamenogorsk, Zaisan, Ayaguz, and of the Semirech'e.

Aḥmad-Walī b. ᶜAlī al-Qazānī (1833-1901)

Both his own history of Semipalatinsk, the *Kitāb-i Tawārīkh-i Sīmīpūlāṭ Qalᶜa* (The History Book of the City of Semipalatinsk) and the manuscript work of Qurbānᶜalī Khālidī contain sufficient biographical information on Aḥmad-Walī to provide us with an idea of his life and career and about his students and successors.

Aḥmad-Walī's full name was Mullā Ākhūnd Aḥmad-Walī b. ᶜAlī b. Munāsib b. Ūrāḍ-Muḥammad al-Qazānī al-Ūtārī. He was born in Semipalatinsk in 1833. His mother's name was ᶜĀ'isha Mūsā qizī, but he provides no information on her dates or origin. His father, who died before Aḥmad-Walī's birth, was from the village of Utar in Kazan province. Aḥmad-Walī tells us he was a merchant, doing business in Tashkent and Bukhara and that he lived at least some time in those cities as a Sufi, studying under local *shaykhs*.

Aḥmad-Walī received his initial education in Semipalatinsk in the *madrasa* of Riḍā'addīn Ḥaḍrat. In this *madrasa* he also studied under Mullā Faḍlallāh Niᶜmatallāh ōghlī, who himself studied in Bukhara and in the *madrasa* of Dāmullā Ibrāhīm Ḥaḍrat in the village of Chalpu (Bugulma district, Samara province). Around 1851 Aḥmad-Walī went to Bukhara, where he remained for twelve years studying various Islamic sciences, including dogma.

In 1863 he was summoned to Semipalatinsk to replace his former teacher, Faḍlallāh Ni^cmatallāh ōghlī, who had passed away while *imām* of that city's Seventh Mosque. Aḥmad-Walī accepted the position, and in 1864 returned from Ufa, where he passed the examinations licensing him as *ākhūnd, mudarris, khaṭīb* and *imām* of the Seventh Mosque. From 1864 until his death Aḥmad-Walī appears to have gained renown particularly as a *madrasa* instructor and Sufi *shaykh*. Qurbān^calī Khālidī describes his *madrasa* as prosperous and as having graduated numerous experts in Qur'ān recitation.

While *imām* in Semipalatinsk Aḥmad-Walī undertook two major pilgrimages. In 1887 he made a pilgrimage to the tombs of his ancestral village of Utar, in Kazan province and to the village of Chalpu, in Samara province, to visit the grave of Dāmullā Ibrāhīm Ḥaḍrat, the instructor of Aḥmad-Walī's instructor, Faḍlallāh Ni^cmatallāh ōghlī. Qurbān^calī writes that in 1901 Aḥmad-Walī departed for the *ḥajj*, but died in the city of Odessa while on his way to Mecca.

In addition to his legacy as a historian, Aḥmad-Walī had numerous students who became *imāms* throughout eastern Kazakhstan. These include the Kazakh *imām* Mullā Aḥmadjān Ālṭāy Bāy ōghlī who served in Semipalatinsk's Sixth Mosque. In the same city's Second Sart Mosque, which served Central Asians, his student, the Chala Kazakh Mullā ^cInāyatallāh served as an unlicensed *imām*. Outside of Semipalatinsk his student Mullā Yūsuf ^cIbādallāh ōghlī Tānābāyef served as *imām* in Ust'-Kamenogorsk. Another of his students, Walī'allāh Anwārof served as *imām* and ran a *madrasa* in the town of Zaisan, on the border with China. Qurbān^calī also notes that Aḥmad-Walī had a son named Mullā Faḍl A^cẓām, who became *imām* in Semipalatinsk's Fourth Mosque.

The *Kitāb-i Tawārīkh-i Sīmīpūlāṭ Qal^ca*, which is reproduced here in facsimile in its entirety, appears to have survived as a unique manuscript and is possibly an autograph. The only copy known to exist is in the private collection of Mirkasyim Usmanov. It contains thirteen folios and is evidently a finished work, judging from the calligraphy and the polished quality of its prose. The language of the work is basically Volga-Ural

Turki, although it contains some Kazakh and Sart dialectal words and forms. The work fits squarely into the genre of the "village" history, which is characterized by a structure that enumerates the mosques of a given town or villages in sequential order, that is, according to their official number, as was Russian administrative practice at that time, and listing the *imāms*, and sometimes *mu'adhdhins*, of each mosque in chronological order.[24] If anything, this structure illustrates to what degree these Muslim historians understood Russian administrative arrangements to be an organic part of their community's history and local pride appears to have been a major motive force in the composition of these histories.

Aḥmad-Walī provides no information on why he wrote his history, although the Kazakhstani historians Khairullin and Khamidullin actually attribute the history (without evidence) to the Tatar theologian and historian Shihābaddīn Marjānī, who allegedly "instructed" Aḥmad-Walī to write the work "on the basis of Marjānī's words."[25] In any case, Aḥmad-Walī tells us early in his narrative that he based his account on oral sources, creating an original work. The use of oral sources is another typical feature of local Muslim histories in the Volga-Ural region. Although the manuscript being published here is the only copy known to exist, at least to the editors, it is likely that other copies did exist at one time. Riḍā'addīn Fakhraddīn ōghlī cites Aḥmad-Walī as his source for his biographical entry on the Semipalatinsk *imām* ᶜĪsā b. Ibrāhīm al-Mangārī (the only figure from Semipalatinsk who receives a separate entry in Fakhraddin ōghlī's biographical dictionary). It is uncertain whether Fakhraddīn ōghlī is citing Aḥmad-Walī's work or a personal correspondence, but his account of ᶜĪsā b. Ibrāhīm corresponds closely to Aḥmad-Walī's.[26]

---

24 For a discussion of the genre of the village history in the context of Russia's Islamic historiography as a whole cf. Frank, ***Muslim Religious Institutions***, 17-36.

25 These authors refer to Aḥmad-Walī as "Akhmetvali Munasypov" and claim him as one of Marjānī's students, but cite no source for any of their statements; cf. G. T. Khairullin, and A. G. Khamidullin, *Tatary (stranitsy istorii i segodniashnii den')*, (Almaty, 1998), 82.

26 Riḍā'addīn Fakhraddīn ōghlī, *Āthār* II/11, 258-259.

History Book of the City of Semipalatinsk*

by Ākhūnd Aḥmad-Walī b. ᶜAlī al-Qazānī

/1b/ In the Name of God, the Merciful, the Compassionate.

Praise be to the Master of the Worlds, who has privileged certain countries in comparison with others with mosques and Friday mosques, with rituals and principles, and who adorned the mosques with *minbars, miḥrābs, imāms*, and *khaṭībs*; who has applied the rules of the rituals through the *ākhūnds* and *muḥtasibs* and the great scholars; and prayers and greetings to His Prophet, who rendered customary the communal prayers in the mosques, which are the finest places and locations, and on his family, and upon his noble and righteous companions.

Now to begin. In 1306 of the *hijra* of the Prophet, the best prayers and salutations upon him, in 1888, this poor man, full of inadequacies, who needs the pardon of God, the mighty merciful grantor of pardon, having the title of *ākhūnd* of Semipalatinsk, the *khaṭīb* and *imām* in the Seventh Mosque, Mullā Aḥmad-Walī as-Sīmīpūlāṭī b. ᶜAlī b. Munāsib b. Ūrāḍ-Muḥammad al-Qazānī al-Ūṭārī, relate according to what I heard from witnesses of the time of the building of Semipalatinsk, that the city of Semipalatinsk is 2,607 *chāqrūms*[27] to the east of the city of Kazan, and borders on the territory of China.

/2a/ The territory of the city of Semipalatinsk was initially inhabited by Kalmyks and Kazakhs who were subjects of the emperor of China. Most of them were nomadic, and had winter encampments. On the site of the city of Semipalatinsk there are still traces of the Kalmyks' camps. Next to the fortress of Semipalatinsk, there is a hillock shaped like a fort. When the earth is dug up, the Kalmyks' bullets, small square shot and equipment, are found.

---

* In the translation the author's marginal notes appear in parentheses while the editors' additions appear in brackets.

27 *Chāqrūm* in Turki texts from Russia generally corresponds to the Russian unit of measurement *versta*, equivalent to 1.06 kilometers.

[The section regarding] the river on which Semipalatinsk is located. Springs gather in the Altay[28] mountains on Chinese territory, many small rivers are formed, and they become a large river and flow toward the southwest. The river is called the Irtysh, and it has a strong current. Its bottom is all made of river stones. On the southeastern sides of the Irtysh there are big mountains. [These include] Dīlbūghtāy Mountain, Āyrūtāy Mountain, and Dūghdūgha Mountain, and in the southwest there are big mountains too, the one called Sīmībūlāṭ and Kōgān Mountain, and others. Some find Kalmyk objects in these mountains: silver vessels, saddles, goblets, knives, bridles, and objects with Kalmyk [or] Chinese writing on them.

Indeed these traces show that initially the territory of Semipalatinsk was originally under the authority of the Chinese throne. Later the Russian emperor's army came from the Omsk and Tobol'sk regions, and gradually conquered [the region]. There were no battles at all, they gained sovereignty over it, and built forts, buildings, and structures. They brought their own people from Russia and settled them. It was a little more than a hundred years ago that the Russians arrived to build Semipalatinsk. Russians /2b/ were the first to come and settle. When they built structures for Semipalatinsk, most of the buildings were made of pine. Even nowadays most of Semipalatinsk's building are made of pine. The reason is because around Semipalatinsk there are many pine forests. In earlier times they were very close by. The forest used to be no more than five *chāqrūms* away. Now it is fifteen *chāqrūms* away. They bring the trees for the structures. At first, among the structures, there were seven that were made of stone. For that reason, in the mouths of the common, this is the origin of the name Semipalatinsk. That is, there were only seven stone buildings, while all of the others were wooden. But nowadays, even though the number of large stone structures is not large, there are some.

---

[28] Although the text reads Ālātaw, it is clear that the author intends Altay.

The soil of the city located below the mountain on the bank of the Irtysh River is sandy, the environs of the city for three or four *chāqrūms* are good flood plains, meadows, and birch groves. Because the soil is sandy, the arable lands thirty to forty *chāqrūms* from the city of Semipalatinsk are bare of trees. There is an extensive forest there called Bilaghach.[29] They are good and excellent lands; the arable land's black clay is good, and the crops are fine. It is very abundant land. At first, before 1870, it was vacant. After that it was purchased for forty silver kopecks a *desiatina*.[30] On the state lands that are still extensive and that also comprise the Bilaghach lands, there are no crops at present. On its vacant lands thousands of horses and many thousands of sheep and cattle belonging to every wealthy person graze. The livestock of hundreds of wealthy men graze there. Some have a thousand horses, others five hundred, and others two or three hundred.

Now, Russians first came to the country of Semipalatinsk, /3a/ and they constructed buildings and structures. After that, Muslims came from Kazan and all of the villages, and saw [it]. Because this [land] was extensive and good, and because there were trading establishments, and because the Kazakh trade was profitable, Muslims came from Kazan and from every village around Kazan, and they built structures on the bank on the upper flow of the Irtysh River and lived there. (As for the Kazakhs, because they were simple and naive, the Tatar merchants would sell a thirty-kopeck piece of fabric for a sheep.) Although they came after the Russians did, the Muslims live up river, thanks to God. It has easily been a hundred years since the arrival of these Muslims.

[The First Mosque]

Now, [some] Muslims came from Kazan voluntarily, and others came to avoid government service [i.e. conscription] and they settled in Semipalatinsk. They [traveled] with the Kazakhs, or went to Tashkent, and conducted trade, and

---

29 The Russian name for this place is Bel' Agash.

30 A *desiatina* was a Russian unit of area equal to 2.7 acres or 1.09 hectares.

became wealthy. After the Muslims gathered together a *maḥalla*, saying, "a mosque is needed to perform the *namāz* communally," the community collected money and the people built a mosque. They built it high, out of wood, and raised up a minaret. This mosque still exists. It is called the First Mosque. At that time the mosque was named the Shafī Mosque, after Shafī Bāy, the most authoritative among the wealthy men in Semipalatinsk. That is, Shafī Āghāy came and went repeatedly, and raised the money for the building, and also because he himself gave most of the money. And this Shafī Bāy Īshim ōghlī was from the village of Mazarbashi,[31] from the people of the Nine Villages in the Kazan region's forest country. At that time there was another very zealous person in Semipalatinsk, named Sāpqūlbāy.

So they appointed an *imām* to this mosque. They appointed Aḥmad-Īshān, who was perfectly trained in Bukhara in the exoteric sciences, and who studied the esoteric sciences in the *khānaqāh* of Khalīfa Ḥusayn (may peace be upon him),[32] /3b/ and who was licensed [in Sufism] by that noble person. This Aḥmad-Īshān was the son of Muḥammad. Muḥammad was the son of ᶜAbdarrazzāq, ᶜAbdarrazzāq the son of Īshmuḥammad. Īshmuḥammad was the son of Taymī, originally from an unknown village called Kötirnäj in the environs of Kazan.[33] Aḥmad-Īshān's father, Muḥammad, himself temporarily took the position of *imām* in Kazan in the

---

[31] This village was located in Kazan district at the headwaters of the Mazarka River.

[32] Probably a reference to Khalīfa Muḥammad Ḥusayn (1784/85-1833/34, who had studied in Samarqand under Khalīfa Ṣiddīq (born between 1727 and 1731), an Indian follower of Mūsā Khān Dahbidī. Khalīfa Ḥusayn was a very influential shaykh who counted among his students numerous prominent Bukharan scholars, as well as figures from the Volga-Ural region; cf. Baxtiyor Babadžanov, "On the history of the Naqšbandīya muğaddidīya in central Māwarā'annahr in the late 18th and early 19th centuries," *Muslim Culture in Russia and Central Asia from the 18th to the Early 20th Centuries* [vol.1] Michael Kemper, Anke von Kügelgen, Dmitriy Yermakov eds. (Berlin, 1996), 400-402.

[33] This village no longer exists. In former times it was located near Kazan in the *Arskaia doroga*, on the bank of the Kazanka River. In Russian sources it appears as Kutemes; cf. R. N. Stepanov, ed. *Pistsovaia kniga Kazanskogo uezda 1602-1603 godov*, (Kazan, 1978), 137, 143.

Fifth Mosque and in the Zangār Mosque[34] for some time serving temporarily as *imām* before he himself obtained the rank of *dāmullā*.[35] He established himself in the Yangi Bistä[36] until he passed away. He was nicknamed Qizil Mullā. The *īshān's* mother was the daughter of a well known person called Chūtāy, ᶜAbdalᶜazīz b. Ṭūqṭāmish b. Būrāsh, who was the first person to print the Qur'ān and other books in Russia.[37]

Aḥmad Īshān had been *imām* for some years, and Shafī Bāy, Sāpqūlbāy, and others were occupied in all sorts of questions regarding the application of the *sharīᶜa*. Since Aḥmad-Īshān's only inclination was Sufism, and since there was a need for a scholar of the exoteric sciences and a jurist, and someone capable of explaining it, Shafī Bāy invited his fellow villager and kinsman from Mazarbashi, Muḥammadyār, the son of Īshmuḥammad [b. Taymī]. This Muḥammadyār Īshmuḥammad ōghlī's Īshmuḥammad and Īshim were both brothers from the same mother. After arriving, Muḥammadyār became a partner to Aḥmad-Īshān, and was *imām* of this mosque.

After a while, the people multiplied, and when [another] *maḥalla* of people was formed, they moved the First Mosque to the edge of the city, and formed a second *maḥalla*. On the site of this mosque the wealthy men made a second, better *maḥalla*, and enlarged it, /4a/ and they finally built a mosque out of wood. This became the Second Mosque.

---

34 Kazan's Fourth Mosque.

35 Shihābaddīn Marjānī gives this figure's name as Mullā Muḥammad b. ᶜAbdarrazzāq b. Īshmuḥammad b. Taymī and his account corresponds very closely with Aḥmad-Walī's; cf. Shihābaddīn al-Marjānī, *Mustafād al-akhbār fī aḥwāl Qazān wa Bulghār* II, (Kazan, 1900), 85, 92.

36 Kazan's "New Tatar Quarter," known in Russian as Novaia Tatarskaia Sloboda.

37 This person appears in Russian sources as Abulgazi Burashev and is credited with founding the first Tatar printing house in Kazan in 1797; cf. Michael Kemper, *Sufis und Gelehrte in Tatarien und Baschkirien: der islamische Diskurs unter russicher Herrschaft, 1789-1889*, (Berlin, 1998), 44-45.

So, Muḥammadyār became *imām* to this First Mosque, that had been moved, and he received his license[38] during the time of the mufti Muḥammadjān.[39] Muḥammadyār was someone who had received training in Bukhara, and who had studied the books to completion. He was a person who was licensed in Sufism by the Ṣāḥibzāda *īshāns*[40] (Ṣāḥibzāda was one of the famous and perfect shaykhs of Bukhara. Currently in his place there is an *īshān* from among his sons.) during the era of Amīr-i Saᶜīd.[41] (Amīr-i Saᶜīd was the ruler of Bukhara. He was a jurist, a *qārī*, and one who had committed the Qur'ān to memory and he was also the ruler. He gave lessons to the students, and had many *shāgirds*.) This Muḥammadyār had studied in Bukhara, and then returned. Then he spent some

---

38 The license, called by its Russian name (*ukaz*) or by its Muslim name (*manshūr*), was conferred upon *ākhūnds*, *imāms* and *mu'adhdhins* by the local provincial authorities after the candidate passed an examination in Ufa given by the Orenburg Spiritual Assembly; cf. Frank, *Muslim Religious Institutions*, 120-133.

39 The first mufti, Muḥammadjān b. al-Ḥusayn (Guseinov or Khuseinov in Russian sources), who served from 1788 until 1824; on this figure cf. Michael Kemper, *Sufis und Gelehrte in Tatarien und Baschkirien*, 50-66; Danil' D. Azamatov, "The Muftis of the Orenburg Spiritual Assembly from the 18th and 19th Centuries: The Struggle for Power in Russia's Muslim Institution," *Muslim Culture in Russia and Central Asia in the 18th to the Early 20th Centuries* vol. 2: Inter-Regional and Inter-Ethnic Relations, Anke von Kügelgen, Michael Kemper, Allen J. Frank eds., (Berlin, 1998), 356-364.

40 The Ṣāḥibzāda *īshāns* is evidently a reference to the successors of Miyān Faḍl Aḥmad, or Ṣāḥibzāda īshān, who was also known as Miyān Aḥmad-i Ṣāḥib. This figure had been initiated into the Mujaddidīya, Qādirīya, Chishtīya, and possibly the Suhrawardīya orders. According to biographical information discussed by Anke von Kügelgen, he originally came from India, probably from Peshawar; cf. Anke von Kügelgen, "Die Entfaltung der Naqšbandīya muǧaddidīya im mittleren Transoxanien vom 18. bis zum Beginn des 19. Jahrhunderts: Ein Stück Detektivarbeit," *Muslim Culture* vol. 2, 128-130; on his legacy in Western Siberia and the northern Kazakh steppe cf. Thierry Zarcone, "Les confréries soufies en Sibérie (XIXe siècle ee début du XXe siècle), *En islam sibérien* (*Cahiers du Monde russe*, 41/2-3, 2000), 287-291.

41 Amīr-i Saᶜīd was an epithet of the Emir of Bukhara Amīr Ḥaydar; cf. von Kügelgen, "Die Entfaltung der Naqšbandīya muǧaddidīya," 135 n. 146; for publications of Miyān Faḍl Aḥmad's correspondence with Amīr Ḥaydar cf. Anke von Kügelgen, "Sufimeister und Herrscher im Zwiegespräch: Die Schreiben des Faḍl Aḥmad aus Peschawar an Amīr Ḥaydar in Buchara," *Muslim Culture in Russia and Central Asia. Vol. 3 Arabic, Persian and Turkic Manuscripts (15th to 19th Centuries)*, Anke von Kügelgen, Aširbek Muminov, Michael Kemper eds. (Berlin, 2000), 219-352.

time in his village Mazarbashi. It was in 1806 that he came [to Semipalatinsk] upon Shafī Bāy's invitation, according to what his son Faḍlallāh said.

Muḥammadyār was *imām* in the First Mosque for a number of years and was giving lessons in his *madrasa*. This son Mullā Faḍlallāh went to Bukhara to study and came back. After that, while he [Muḥammadyār] was still healthy, his son Mullā Faḍlallāh became *imām*. There was no teaching in the First Mosque during the time of Mullā Faḍlallāh. In the *madrasa khalfas* and children's teachers were giving lessons. Then Mullā Faḍlallāh [alone] was *imām* for a number of years. After that, his son Muḥammad-ᶜAlīm Makhdūm, who had studied for a few years with Dāmullā Ismāᶜīl Mudarris[42] in the village of Qishqar,[43] which is in the environs of Kazan, returned [to Semipalatinsk], received his official license after three or four years, and became *imām*. Later the people did not like him, and removed him. In 1882, Mullā Yahūda Abū Bakr ōghlī, who was born in Semipalatinsk, and who was nicknamed ᶜUthmān Qārī, became *imām*. This Mullā Yahūda had studied in Bukhara, and had read the *ḥikmat al-ᶜayn*,[44] and he returned to his homeland. He was a shopkeeper in Semipalatinsk /4b/ and Chuguchak, [then] became a merchant and traveled around. Then in 1882 he obtained his official license for the First Mosque and became the *imām*. Currently the name of the *imām* in Semipalatinsk's First Mosque is Mullā Yahūda. His nickname is ᶜUthmān Qārī, and he is the son of Abū Bakr b. Shafī Bāy.

Since the construction of the First Mosque there have been four *imāms* here. First Muḥammadyār, second, his son Mullā Faḍlallāh, third his son Muḥammad-ᶜAlīm, fourth Mullā

---

42 Ismāᶜīl b. Mūsā al-Machkarawī al-Qishqārī (d. 1887/88); cf. Muḥammad Murād ar-Ramzī, *Talfīq al-akhbār wa-talqīḥ al-āthār fī waqā'iᶜ Qazān wa-Bulġār wa-mulūk at-Tatār* II, (Orenburg, 1908), 478.

43 Officially known as Kshkar, this village is today located in Arsk *raion*, Tatarstan.

44 This anonymous work was evidently a common philosophical text in the *madrasas* of Imperial Russia; cf. Frank, *Muslim Religious Institutions*, 244.

Yahūda, who is called ᶜUthmān Qārī. Since the construction of this mosque, there have been six *mu'adhdhins* here. First, Bashīr Mu'adhdhin, second Raḥmatallāh Mu'adhdhin, third Saydāsh Mu'adhdhin, fourth Sayyid-ᶜAlī Mu'adhdhin b. Saydāsh, fifth Ḥasan Mu'adhdhin b. Muḥammadyār, sixth Aḥmad-Shāh Mu'adhdhin b. Sayyid-ᶜAlī. At present this Ḥasan, together with Aḥmad-Shāh, are healthy and do the job of *mu'adhdhin*.

[The Second Mosque]

And so, Shafī Bāy and Sāpqūlbāy built a second, and better, wooden mosque in their *maḥalla*. Aḥmad-Īshān became *imām* in this Second Mosque. After many years, when Aḥmad-Īshān had grown old, his son Ibrāhīm Makhdūm went to Bukhara, and returned, after spending two or three years there in rectitude. He obtained an official license and became *imām* in Aḥmad-Īshān's place. (It was during the time of the Ufa mufti Salīm-Girāy Tawkīlef).[45] After a number of years, he attained the rank of *ākhūnd*, when the Russian rulers in Semipalatinsk made him the Chief *ākhūnd* without [taking] an examination; so he was called Ākhūnd. Later, Mullā ᶜUbaydallāh Dāmullā ᶜAbdalfayḍ ōghlī came from the city of Kazan and married the daughter of Ibrāhīm Aḥmad ōghlī. Because he was his son-in-law (house son-in-law),[46] while Ibrāhīm Ākhūnd was in good health, Mullā ᶜUbaydallāh took the examination [in Ufa], received an official license, and became the *mu'adhdhin* and *imām*-designate. After Ibrāhīm Ākhūnd's death, a new /5a/ confirmation was again put together, and he became *imām* of this Second stone Mosque. Presently he is the *imām*. It is known that the mosque Shafī Bāy had built burned down and was destroyed in the 1840's or so.

Subsequently, Aḥmad-Īshān made a request of the late and well-known Mūsā Bāy from the village of Qishqar, and with

---

45 The fourth Orenburg mufti, r. 1865-1885, known in Russian sources as Salimgarei Tevkelev.

46 That is, a son-in-law who lived with his wife's parents.

his guidance, he [Mūsā Bāy] gave thirty thousand rubles in copper, and [they] began building a stone mosque. Those thirty thousand rubles did not suffice, and when Mūsā Bāy did not give more money a second time, there was a tyrannical police chief in Semipalatinsk at that time named Vasil'evich. Joining with him [Aḥmad-Īshān] he [Vasil'evich], whose name was doubly terrifying, said, "The mosque that was begun shall not stay a meadow," and also saying that is an example of the adornment and flowering of the city. This tyrannical police chief thought about his intention and he frightened all of the wealthy men at that time. He made some of them think by constraint and force, and speaking to all of them, he said to some, "Give a thousand," and to others, "Give three hundred rubles," and by doing that and making his wishes known, he berated and insulted them and he collected the money from the rich men. In order to complete the stone mosque that had been begun, all of the wealthy men of Semipalatinsk were berated and they contributed. (It was heard from some of the wealthy men themselves, who said, "In this way we were cursed and berated, and we gave.") The old *imāms* of Semipalatinsk tell this story, saying, "They feared the Russian [police chief] would bring constraint and distress, and the Second stone Mosque was built from the money that was contributed." A beautiful and quite tall stone mosque appeared, and next to it there is a *maktab*. It was [also] built out of stone, and has two rooms. In 1882 /5b/ Muḥammad-Ṣiddīq Bāy b. Muḥammad-Ṣādiq Bāy b. Rafīq Bāy, who was living in Semipalatinsk, built the structure from his own funds. It was used for teaching children.

Since the construction of Semipalatinsk's Second Mosque, there have been three *imāms* here. First, Aḥmad-Īshān, second Ibrāhīm Ākhūnd, third Mullā ᶜUbaydallāh b. Dāmullā ᶜAbdalfayḍ. Currently this one is [*imām*]. Since the construction of this mosque there have been six *mu'adhdhins*. First, Waddallāh, second Sayfaddīn Mu'adhdhin, third Walī Mullā Mu'adhdhin, fourth Ismāᶜīl Mu'adhdhin b. Aḥmad-Īshān, fifth, Jalāladdīn Mu'adhdhin b. Ismāᶜīl Mu'adhdhin, sixth Shāhī Mardān Mu'adhdhin. The latter two are currently in good health.

[The Third Mosque]

Muslims were coming from everywhere, from Kazan and from its environs. Some came voluntarily, and others came as fugitives, changing their names and settling in Semipalatinsk. After enough people for a mosque and a *maḥalla* had gathered, a merchant from the village of Mangar, Ṭāhir, and his younger brother, Ibrāhīm, the sons of ᶜAbdallaṭīf, built the large wooden Third Mosque, with their own money. This Ṭāhir was nicknamed Bōṭā Ṭāhir. He was a good and generous person. The origin of his nickname is as follows: Bōṭā Ṭāhir had an older brother named Ḥamīd. He was someone whose build and height was very great. They would do business among the Kazakhs. The Kazakhs are a people who have a strong taste for distorting a person's name and giving him a nickname. Since Ḥamīd was a very tall person, they gave him the nickname Tōye Ḥamīd [Camel Ḥamīd]. They also gave his younger brother Ṭāhir the nickname Bōṭā. Bōṭā means the offspring of a camel.

/6a/ The construction of this third mosque was in 1837. Dāmullā ᶜĪsā Ībrāhīm ōghlī, from the village of Ulugh Mangar,[47] who had studied in Bukhara, and had studied the books and the Sufi path, became *imām* in the Third Mosque. Next to the mosque was a three-room wooden *madrasa* that Ṭāhir Bāy had built. After this building became old and dilapidated, in 1877 everyone from the community collected money, and [with] Qārī Aḥmad-Ṣafā being the *imām*, a *madrasa* was built out of stone. Currently this is the structure. This Dāmullā ᶜĪsā was a good person and a pious Sufi. He was [easily] satisfied, and at times he would say to those bringing offerings and tithes "Right now I have food and the things [I need]. This belongs to the poor. Give this to other

---

[47] Officially known as Bol'shoi Menger, today located in Atnia *raion*, Tatarstan.

poor people." He wouldn't accept offerings and would give them back.

Later, in 1862, after the death of Dāmullā ᶜĪsā, Qārī Aḥmad-Ṣafā al-Muḥammad Mullā ōghlī, who was from a village near the city of Chistopol'[48] and who had studied the books to completion in Bukhara, became *imām*. Later, after he died, his younger brother [of the same mother], Mullā Muḥsīn Mullā al-Muḥammad ōghlī in 1882 became *imām* to the Third Mosque. Presently it is this person [who is *imām*].

Now, he is the third *imām* here since the construction of this Third Mosque: first, Mullā ᶜĪsā, second Qārī Aḥmad-Ṣafā, third Mullā Muḥsin. There have been four *mu'adhdhins* here since the construction of this mosque: first, Iḥsān Mu'adhdhin, second, Muḥammad-Ṣādiq Mu'adhdhin b. Iḥsān, third Ṣāliḥ Mu'adhdhin, fourth ᶜAbdaljabbār Mu'adhdhin b. Ṣāliḥ Mu'adhdhin. Currently he is in good health.

[The Fourth Mosque]

After that, the city of Semipalatinsk /6b/ grew some more, the people multiplied, and when at the far end of the city there were enough people to make up a *maḥalla*, saying, "We find that the mosque is too far away," the people gathered, collected money, and built the Fourth Mosque. It was a large wooden mosque, and in 1847, Dāmullā Riḍā'addīn, who had studied in Bukhara and studied the books and the Sufi path and who was a learned jurist, and an excellent, godly, and pious person, became *imām* to this mosque. He took the examination from ᶜAbdalwāḥid Muftī,[49] was a handsome person, with a fine appearance, and good moral virtues displayed by actions. He had pleasant disposition and fine conversational skills; in the *madrasa* he had many *shāgirds* and gave lessons, and he passed his life [in that way]. This fine man passed away in 1879. May God have mercy on him. Amen.

---

48 Formerly a district seat in Kazan province, today a *raion* center in Tatarstan.

49 The third Orenburg mufti, ᶜAbdalwāḥid b. Sulaymān (1840-1862), known in Russian cources as Gabdulvakhid Suleimanov.

Mullā Aḥmadjān ᶜUbaydallāh ōghlī, the *mu'adhdhin* and assistant *imām*, who came from the Kazan region and who in his youth had studied for a while in Qishqar under Yaᶜqūb Ḥaḍrat,[50] took [Dāmullā Riḍā'addīn's] place and after his death collected a confirmation and was put in the position of *imām*. Presently this [person] is *imām*.

There have been two *imāms* since the construction of this Fourth Mosque: first, Dāmullā Riḍā'addīn Walīd ōghlī and second, Mullā Aḥmadjān b. ᶜUbaydallāh. Since the construction of the Fourth Mosque there have been four *mu'adhdhins*: first, Nuᶜman Mu'adhdhin, who was a *sunnatchī bābāy*[51] from the village of Masra,[52] second, ᶜAbdalghafūr Mu'adhdhin, third Aḥmadjān Mu'adhdhin, fourth ᶜAlīm Mu'adhdhin.

[The Fifth Mosque]

The Fifth Mosque is a wooden mosque without a minaret, that a wealthy Kazakh named Jūlāmān built in 1827 on the southern side of Semipalatinsk, on the south side of the Irtysh River.[53] Mullā ᶜAbdalkarīm b. Abū Bakr, from the village of Kugarchin,[54] /7a/ who had studied the sciences in Bukhara, and had trained in Samarqand and studied the books to perfection, became the unlicensed *imām* for this mosque. Now this Mullā ᶜAbdalkarīm's moral character did not suit the Kazakhs, and the Kazakhs did not suit him either, so after remaining a year or two, he resigned.

After that, the Mullā Muḥammad-Amīn Manṣūrof, from the Nizhnii Novgorod Mishars, who had trained for a short time in

---

50 Yaᶜqūb b. Yaḥyā at-Tubyāzī; cf. Riḍā'addīn Fakhraddīn ōghlī, *Āthār*, II/10, 128.

51 That is, one who specializes in performing circumcision.

52 This village was officially known as Masry, and was located in Kazan district.

53 The suburb of Dzhulamanka, on the south bank of the Irtysh, was evidently named after this Jūlāmān Bāy.

54 There were at least two villages named Kugarchin in the Volga-Ural region in the nineteenth century; one located in Kazan province's Laishevo district, and the other located in Ufa province's Birsk district.

Machkara with the famous Dāmullā ᶜAbdallāh Mudarris,[55] and who had studied Qur'ān recitation with Ādā'ī Ḥaḍrat,[56] became *imām*. After that, after the minaretless mosque grew dilapidated, old, and rotted, in 1876 the people and the wealthy men built a fine large wooden mosque for the community in its place. Since the building of this mosque, the *imām* has remained and is currently Muḥammad-Amīn. Next to the mosque a three-room wooden *madrasa* was built. It was with the money of the sponsor, notable, and patron of the *ᶜulamā*, Tlāw Bāy Ābdān ōghlī, who was a Kazakh and who resided in this *maḥalla*. Instruction in the sciences is carried out [there].

In 1887 they gave the *imām* a co-*imām*. [This was] Mullā Ḥusāmaddīn Mullā Zaynalᶜābidīn ōghlī from Semipalatinsk, who became co-*imām* and *imām*-designate. He was the deputy when the imām Muḥammad-Amīn was absent. ([Also] when Muḥammad-Amīn was present he was the deputy).

This Fifth Mosque is on the bank of the Irtysh River. Currently most of the people [in the *maḥalla*] are Kazakhs. There are five or six who are merchants, *meshchane*,[57] or wealthy men, and the rest are all Kazakhs. In all, rich and poor make up more than five hundred households and it is a large settlement. Most of the houses have flat roofs and just holes for windows. But even if the fundamentals [of religious practice] are inexact, they gather firmly for the communal prayers /7b/ and how bad are their ablutions! They do not wash properly, and in wiping the fingertips, they just wet them lightly. They go to the mosque, and say, "May God accept it." Their *imāms* give them much instruction.

Since the building of the Fifth Mosque, there have been two *mu'adhdhins*. The first was the *mu'adhdhin* named Walīd, from the time of the above-mentioned Jūlāmān Mosque, which

---

55 ᶜAbdallāh b. Yaḥyā b. Maḥmūd al-Machkarawī; cf. Riḍā'addīn Fakhraddīn ōghlī, *Āthār*, II/12 No.349.

56 Ṭāhir b. Subḥānqul b. Bahādirshāh al-Ādā'ī; cf. Riḍā'addīn Fakhraddīn ōghlī, *Āthār*, II/13 No. 387.

57 In imperial Russia *meshchane*, primarily merchants and landowners, were constituted as a formal estate (*soslovie*).

lacked a minaret. He died after reaching the age of 110. He was the father of Dāmullā ᶜAlī, who was the *imām* in Ust'-Kamenogorsk. The second *mu'adhdhin* was ᶜAbdallāh Mu'adhdhin.

[The Sixth Mosque]

The Sixth Mosque was built in 1829, close to this *maḥalla* [of the Fifth Mosque], on the riverbank. It was wooden, without a minaret, [and was built by] the Kazakh Tinūbāy Kōkān ōghlī.[58] This *maḥalla* was entirely made up of Kazakhs as well, and numbered about 150 houses. The *imām* of this mosque is the Kazakh Mullā Aḥmadjān Ālṭāy Bāy ōghlī. He studied the sciences in Semipalatinsk under Ākhūnd Mullā Aḥmad-Walī. During the time of Salīm-Girāy Muftī, he took the exam in Ufa and became a licensed *imām*. There is also a *maktab* next to the mosque. It is used for teaching children. Since the construction of this mosque there have been three *imāms*: first, a Kazakh *mullā* named Bābājān, second, one named Niᶜmatjān, from Ufa district. The third (current) *imām* is Mullā Aḥmadjān b. Ālṭāy Bāy.

The builder of the mosque was Tinūbāy Kōkānof Ḥājjī. He was a very generous man. He was renowned for kindness to travelers, and munificence to guests and friends, and his wealth was very great. His wealth remained until the end of his life. He died in 1887 at the age of 98. May the mercy of God be upon him. He left no male heir. All of his sons had died while he was alive. But a single elderly daughter remained. She had an unrighteous and impious /8a/ husband. He was the Kazakh Ibrāhīm Nurākān ōghlī. That unrighteous Ibrāhīm took the property, but at the time of his death there was little left compared to [what there had been] in former times. The late Tinūbāy Ḥājjī, while he was sound in body, did good and pious deeds. He gave offerings and diverted them to their [rightful] place. He turned the tall buildings next to the

---

58 This wealthy Kazakh appears in Russian sources as Tynybai Kevkhinev, and in 1839 became a merchant of the Third Guild; cf. Kasymbaev, *Istoriia goroda Semipalatinska*, 97.

mosque, as well as the lots, into *waqfs*. May God accept them. Amen.

[The Seventh Mosque]

In the city of Semipalatinsk the population continued to grow, and another *mahalla* came into being. They built the Seventh Friday Mosque out of wood. It was built in 1852 with money the people had collected themselves. There was an *imām* for this mosque, Mullā Zaynalᶜābidīn ᶜAbdalmannān ōghlī, [who] studied the books to completion in Bukhara and [was] originally from the village of Machkara (this Dāmullā Zaynalᶜābidīn was a diligent scholar and a keen debater and was very intelligent). After Mullā Zaynalᶜābidīn had been *imām* for three or four years, he became afflicted with paralysis. He gave up the position of *imām* , and lived another five years. At that time the *mu'adhdhin*, Muṣṭafā Saᶜīd ōghlī became *imām* and carried out [the duties].

Then in 1863 Mullā Faḍlallāh Niᶜmatallāh ōghlī, who had studied in Bukhara, and was from Ufa district (or Bugul'ma district), from a village named Suqayïsh (on the Ik River),[59] near the village of Chalpu,[60] became *imām* (In the city of Semipalatinsk, during the time of Dāmullā Riḍā'addīn, Mullā Faḍlallāh was the master to the author, as *khalfa*). Before going to Bukhara, this person [Faḍlallāh] studied in the village of Chalpu under the renowned Dāmullā Ibrāhīm Ḥaḍrat[61] (In 1887, when this poor author went to this master of masters, Dāmullā Ibrāhīm Ḥaḍrat, and was a guest in the village of Chalpu, I visited his tomb. It was the place of great works). Mullā Faḍlallāh took the examination during the time of Salīm-Girāy Muftī. When he had obtained the official license, he

[59] Officially known as Sukhaesh, this village was located in Bugul'ma district, Samara province; today it is located in Aznakaevo *raion*, Tatarstan.

[60] Officially known as Chalpy, this village was also located in Bugul'ma district, Samara province; today it is likewise located in Aznakaevo *raion*, Tatarstan.

[61] Ibrāhīm is mentioned by Muḥammad-Salīm Umitbaev's list of the prominent scholars inhabiting the Bashkir lands; cf. Muḥammad-Salīm Umīdbāyef, *Yādigār*, (Kazan, 1897), 107-108; cf also Riḍā'addīn Fakhraddīn ōghlī, *Āthār*, II/11, 214.

returned to Semipalatinsk; during a Friday prayer in this mosque, he performed the *khuṭba* in a state of illness, and took to his sickbed. He died after a month or two. It was the flux. May God have mercy upon him.

After his death, the people summoned me, the poor author of this history, from Bukhara, /8b/ saying, "Come back, in order to become *imām*." At that time I had been in rectitude in Bukhara for twelve years, and had studied the books to completion. Initially, in Semipalatinsk, I had studied dogma with Dāmullā Riḍā'addīn, [then] I went to Bukhara, further studied dogma, and our master in the science of dogma was Dāmullā Najmaddīn, may peace be upon him. We completed our studies that year, and our master in the lesson of questions was Dāmullā Niyāz Balkhī, may peace be upon him.[62] And when we were taken as deputies of the Sufi order by Miyān Fārūq, the son of Ḥaḍrat-i Kalān Ṣāḥibzāda Ḥaḍrat, we received our license and returned [to Semipalatinsk]. In that year we went to the place for the examination in the city of Ufa, and took the examination during the time of Salīm-Girāy Muftī, and passed. Those administering the exam said, "You merit the position of *ākhūnd*," and they gave me the diploma for *ākhūnd, mudarris, khaṭīb* and *imām*. So, in 1864, along with that diploma and the people's confirmation, I received the license for the Seventh Friday mosque, and became the *mudarris, khaṭīb, and ākhūnd*. I am poor Mullā Aḥmad-Walī b. ᶜAlī b. Munāsib b. Ūrāḍ-Muḥammad al-Ūṭārī. (The author Mullā Aḥmad-Walī was born in Semipalatinsk in 1833. My father died when I was in the womb of my late mother ᶜĀ'isha Mūsā qizī and I was born about two months after my father's death. My father was originally from the village of Utar.[63] He came to Semipalatinsk, then would go to Tashkent and Bukhara to trade, and in that abode of saints would sit and keep company with the perfect shaykhs, and he was made a deputy [to a shaykh.]) (The village of Utar is a fine village with a

---

62 We have been unable to further identify either of these two Bukharan figures.

63 Officially known as Utar-Aty and formerly located in Kazan district, Kazan province, this village is today located in Arsk *raion*, Tatarstan.

beautiful spring in the Kazan region, fifteen *chāqrūms* from Ulugh Mangar and three *chāqrūms* from Urnashbash.[64] In 1887 I went and saw Utar when I visited the [tombs of the] ancestors, and called upon my relatives).

And next to this mosque, in that same year [1864] there was a three-room *madrasa* made out of wood. (The *madrasa's* first builder was someone named Fat Ibrāhīm of Semipalatinsk, the younger brother of the well known Rafīq Bāy of Sarda.[65] After that, when it had gotten old, Muḥammadjān Bīkbavīch was the builder of a modern three-room wooden *madrasa*. He was originally from Baylar Orisi,[66] but Semipalatinsk was his home.) For many years we have been well occupied with giving lessons to the gatherings of *shāgirds*, and in 1884, when a [new] *madrasa* was needed, a fine and lofty two-room *madrasa* was built out of stone. Muḥammad-Muṣṭāfā Bāy [had it built], may God accept it, with money bequeathed by the late Muḥammad-Wāṣil Ḥājjī Bāy Murtaḍā ōghlī Khōja-Sayyidof, and with Muḥammad-Yūsuf, the son of Muḥammad-Wāṣil Ḥājjī Bāy. Amen. /9a/ At present *shāgirds* gather there in substantial numbers and I am occupied in giving instruction.

Since the building of the Seventh Mosque, there have been three *imāms* here. [The *imāms* are] first Mullā Zaynal^{c}ābidīn, second Mullā Faḍlallāh, third Mullā Aḥmad-Walī Ākhūnd, the author of this history. This person [is *imām*] at present. Thanks and praise to God, the Lord of the two worlds. And since the building of this Seventh Mosque, there have been three *mu'adhdhins* here. First Thābit Mullā Mu'adhdhin, second Muṣṭafā Mu'adhdhin, third Muḥammadjān Mu'adhdhin b. Muṣṭafā Mu'adhdhin. At present this [person is the *mu'adhdhin*].

---

64 Officially known as Urnashbash and formerly located in Kazan district, Kazan province, this village is today located in Arsk *raion*, Tatarstan.

65 The text is unclear here. Another possible, but less likely, reading is "the Sart Rafīq Bāy."

66 Officially known as Uria and formerly located in Tsarevokokshaisk district, Kazan province, this village is today located in the Mari Republic.

[The Eighth Mosque]

Then people came from all over, and because they settled in Semipalatinsk, in 1859, when there were enough people for another mosque, a rich man named ᶜAṭiyatallāh had a wooden mosque built (with his own money). Mullā Ḥusāmaddin, from the village of Qaz Ile[67] in the environs of Kazan became *imām* of this mosque. He had studied a little in the villages around Kazan, and was a fine old man of good character In Semipalatinsk his nickname was Pisī Mullā [Cat Mullā]. (What I have heard on the origins of this name is the following: when Mullā Ḥusāmaddīn was first in Semipalatinsk, he worked as a butcher. Next door was a girl named Khadīcha, who was the daughter of someone named Baqā-Bashīr [Frog Bashīr] and Khadīcha had a pet cat. When the cat would visit the butcher shop [attracted by] the smell of the meat, Mullā Ḥusāmaddīn would attach a note on the cat's tail greeting Khadīcha. In the end he married Khadīcha and Khadīcha became an *ābiṣṭāy*.)[68]

After this person had been *imām* for a number of years and had grown old, the Mishar, Mullā ᶜAbdaljabbār ᶜUbaydallāh ōghlī, studied the sciences in Bukhara, and studied the books and the Sufi path. Mullā ᶜAbdaljabbār ᶜUbaydallāh ōghlī by chance was returning from Bukhara via Semipalatinsk. When he returned to Semipalatinsk, he married the daughter of Mullā Ḥusāmaddīn, and he taught for a number of years in the *madrasa*, became the *imām*-designate, and received his license; and after Mullā Ḥusāmaddīn died, he became *imām*, *khaṭīb*, and *mudarris*. There is a *madrasa* next to this mosque. During the time of Mullā ᶜAbdaljabbār it was a fine place for studies. Later, Mullā ᶜAbdaljabbār went on the *ḥajj*, and in 1881, when he was on his way back, by God's will he died during the time of quarantine in Turkey.

---

67 Officially known as Kazylino and formerly located in Kazan district, Kazan province, this village is today located in Arsk *raion*, Tatarstan.

68 That is, the wife of an *imām*; on the role of the *abïstay* in Islamic education cf. Frank, *Muslim Religious Institutions*, 226.

/9b/ After this, each of the *mu'adhdhins* and *shāgirds* in the Eighth Mosque [temporarily] became *imām*. This was because the late Mullā ᶜAbdaljabbār had a son who studied in Bukhara. The community waited for eight years, saying, "We'll wait and make him *imām*." They made everyone [an interim] *imām*, and this Mullā Ṣalāḥaddīn, the son of the late Mullā ᶜAbdaljabbār would say, "I'll be returning from Bukhara," and he made the community wait for a year or two. After that, according to the saying, "The loyalty of the common people is well known," various things were heard, and even though the poor son returned from his travels, there was already another student who longed for the rank of *imām*, therefore he was very much longing [for the position]. As a result of every sort of intrigue and scandal and enmity toward one another, he told the community, "I will become the co-*imām* to the Third Mosque." So they made someone named ᶜAbdalḥaqq *imām*, who had greatly bothered the *imām* of that mosque. He was originally from Tiumen', (and had studied for three or four years in Istanbul). Presently he is the *imām*.

So, in the Eighth Mosque there were three *imāms*: first, Mullā Ḥusāmaddīn, second Mullā ᶜAbdaljabbār, and third Mullā ᶜAbdalḥaqq b. Mullā ᶜImādaddīn. And since the building of this mosque there has been a single *mu'adhdhin*, Ṣafī'allāh Mu'adhdhin b. Saydāsh Mu'adhdhin. Currently this Ṣafī'allāh [is *mu'adhdhin*].

[The Ninth Mosque]

The population and the community increased, and in 1882 Muḥammadjān Ḥājjī Ismāᶜīl ōghlī Īshtirākof, who was originally from the village of Tashkichü,[69] built the Ninth Mosque with his own money. Mullā Kamāladdīn Muḥammad-Raḥīm ōghlī, from the environs of Kazan, became *imām* of this mosque. He initially studied in Qishqar, and after that spent three years in Bukhara and received training. And ᶜUbayd Mu'adhdhin is *mu'adhdhin* in this mosque. There is

---

69 Officially called Tashkichu, this village was located in Kazan district, Kazan province, and is today located in Arsk *raion*, Tatarstan.

also /10a/ a *madrasa* next to it. At present he is occupied in teaching, and has *shāgirds*. He compiles the official registers[70] for the Spiritual Assembly.

The number of mosques in Semipalatinsk is nine. One of them is stone, and the rest are made of pine. The five daily prayers and the Friday prayers are performed in all of them. The community is large. There is one *imām* each for every one of the mosques. They are not co-*imāms*. However in some of the *mu'adhdhins'* licenses, it is written that they have the position of *imām*.[71]

In addition to these mosques, there are two other mosques in Semipalatinsk. They are called the Sarts' mosques. One of them was built at the time the First Mosque was built in Semipalatinsk. Sarts came from Tashkent and set up residence in Semipalatinsk. They married women and girls from among the Kazakhs, and they remained in Semipalatinsk (It is also called the Chala Kazakhs' *maḥalla*).[72] They didn't return to Tashkent and they built a small mosque without a minaret. It had a Tashkentian-style exterior and appearance. The common people called this mosque the Toqal Mosque.[73] This is evidently because it has no minaret. In 1888 the builder of this mosque was around ninety years old. They made a Sart, who was called a Chala Kazakh, Mullā ᶜInāyatallāh, the *imām* to

---

70 In Russian, *metricheskie knigi*, registers of births, deaths and marriages in a specific *maḥalla*.

71 That is, such a *mu'adhdhin* had legal authority to carry out the duties of an *imām*; on the institution of the *mu'adhdhin* in imperial Russia cf. Frank, *Muslim Religious Institutions*, 146-151.

72 Chala Kazakhs were Muslims primarily descended from Kazakh mothers and Central Asian or Tatar fathers who had come to Kazakhstan. Chala Kazakhs were distinguished from Kazakhs genealogically, that is, since their fathers were not Kazakhs, they were not part of the Kazakh kinship system. They were also distinguished from Tatars since the Russian authorities recognized them as "*inorodtsy*," (natives) while Tatars were for the most part state peasants, meaning that Tatars were subject to the poll tax and military service, while the Chala Kazakhs were not. However, many Tatars, who were not descended from Kazakh mothers, were registered as Chala Kazakhs, avoiding the poll tax and military service; such figures include Qurbānᶜalī Khālidī; cf. Qurbānᶜalī Khālidī, *Tawārīkh-i khamsa-yi sharqī*, 384-391.

73 Literally "the Polled Mosque" or the "Hornless Mosque."

this Toqal Mosque, and he became an unlicensed *imām* on his own volition. He was educated in Semipalatinsk by Ākhūnd Mullā Aḥmad-Walī and is a pious person.

The Second Sarts' Mosque was built at the expense of the Tashkentian Mīr-Qurbān Bāy Awwāb Bāy ōghlī, who resided in Semipalatinsk. Mīr-Qurbān Bāy was nicknamed Būqāsh.[74] As for this mosque, it has two good and large minarets. This ornamented mosque was made of wood. The *imām* in the mosque was a Sart, /10b/ Mullā Aḥmadjān Qārī b. Mullā Muslim b. Mu'minjān Bāy. This Aḥmadjān Qārī was the *qārī* and *ḥāfiẓ* in the mosque of Ākhūnd Mullā Aḥmad-Walī in Semipalatinsk. He studied for a short time, and became *imām* to this mosque.

There are no *madrasas* or *maktabs* adjacent to these two mosques. The children of these Sarts go to the other *madrasas* for reading. Furthermore, these two mosques are not given *metricheskie knigi* from the Spiritual Assembly. *Pamiatnye knigi* are given from [the administration] of Semipalatinsk district.[75] In these the births, deaths, marriages and divorces are recorded, and the books are submitted [to the administration]. The communities are under the authority of the Tashkentian and Kazakh administration. Currently they do not provide conscripts, [but] they pay the *chāngārāq* tax, that is the smoke tax.[76] Earlier there were very many rich men among these Sart Chala-Kazakhs. Now all of them are poor. Some of the children of the rich men who were incomparably wealthy moved to Russia and others to China. In the wealthy times, their moral qualities [were such that even] before the morning

---

74 In Russian sources he appears as Mirkurban Niiazov, and was also the headman (*āqsaqāl*) of the Central Asian community in Semipalatinsk; cf. Qurbānᶜalī Khālidī, *Tawārīkh-i khamsa-yi sharqī*, 366-367.

75 In this sense, the Sart community differed institutionally from the Tatars, Kazakhs, and Chala Kazakhs. Whereas the Kazakhs, Chala Kazakhs and Tatars submitted their registers to the Orenburg Muslim Spiritual Assembly, the Sarts, as former subjects of the Central Asian khanates, submitted their registers to the Semipalatinsk provincial authorities.

76 Literally the "smoke-hole tax," formerly levied on every yurt; in effect it was a hearth tax, levied on every household, and was paid by *inorodtsy* in lieu of the poll tax.

prayers they would go to their windows [to pray]. Nowadays, in summertime they sleep in until eleven o'clock, out of sloth.

So, in Semipalatinsk there are a total of eleven Friday mosques. Two of them are on the far side of the river, two of them belong to the Sarts, and of the seven [remaining] one is stone, while the rest are wooden. In every one of them the five daily prayers and the Friday prayers and the *ᶜīd* prayers are performed. In some years [the *ᶜīd* prayers] are performed in each of the mosques, and in other years [people] assemble by the stone mosque, where a broad space is fenced off. And on the steppe [as] there is no public place for prayer in conformity with what has been established, various people come, saying, "[Let us] gather." This humble man performs [the prayers] in our own mosque with many people, and the others perform them in their own mosques. And none of these mosques /11a/ are located among the Russians. Upriver the houses of some in the Muslim community are located among some of the Russians, but their streets do not mix their smoke.[77] However, the smoke of the community of the Eighth Mosque, which is called the ᶜAtiyatallāh Mosque of which ᶜAbdalḥaqq is *imām*, does mingle with the Russians' smoke.

Furthermore, in Semipalatinsk, in every case, all of the mosques that were built by a wealthy man go by the name of that wealthy man. For example, the Third Mosque is the Bōṭā Mosque, that is, Ṭāhir Bāy, nicknamed Bōṭā, built [it]. They call the Eighth Mosque the ᶜAtiyatallāh Mosque and the Ninth Mosque the Īshtirākof Mosque. They name the mosques built with the money of the community after their *imāms*. For example, the Riḍā Ḥaḍrat Mosque, the Muḥammadyār Ḥaḍrat Mosque, the Mullā Aḥmad-Walī Ākhūnd Mosque, and so forth.

Thanks and praise be to God, in the city of Semipalatinsk there are many mosques, and in each of the mosques there are many

---

77 Aḥmad-Walī seems to be indicating that even in the Russian districts of the city, Muslim and Russians lived along separate streets.

people with turbans for each *namāz*, and especially for the Friday prayers there are very many people [present].

By the Sart Mosque, the Būqāsh Mosque, there is a treasured beard hair of the Prophet Muḥammad, may peace be upon him, which they keep in a special location, in a special room in the house of Būqāsh. It was put in a special room inside the guest room and it was put there with special attention, let there be thanks. When a Dungan [who was] a holy *shaykh*, an *īshān*, a *ṣāḥib-i nafas*[78] and a *ṣāḥib-i karāmat*[79] was in Istanbul while returning from the *ḥajj*, he received it from the Sultan ᶜAbdalmajīd,[80] because he cured the Sultan's mother of illness when she was ill. When the mother of Sultan ᶜAbdalmajīd /11b/ offered the *īshān* all sorts of jewels and gold from their worldly possessions, he turned them down and requested a single item from the treasury, the blessed hair, and he received two blessed items, and in Semipalatinsk he gave them to Būqāsh Bāy. He went again on the *ḥajj*, and he died on the way back. It was in a Muslim village containing two mosques named Jawkeldi,[81] between Kazan and Irbit. Now it has become a place of pilgrimage, and there are some miracles for the pilgrims. They say that a red-green tree grew at the head of his grave. They say we have never seen the likes of that tree in any province. One travelers' account states that it is a wondrous tree whose leaves stay green all winter and all summer. Praise God.[82]

Indeed, there are illustrious things in Semipalatinsk. There is an abundance of mosques and Muslims, and a blessed hair of our Prophet Muḥammad, may peace be upon him. The people are humble and have no haughty qualities, and if in their life

78 A healer; cf. Frank, *Muslim Religious Institutions*, 144.
79 A Muslim saint; one capable of performing miracles.
80 That is, Sultan Abdülmecit I.
81 Officially this village was known as Iavgeldin, and was located in Birsk district, Ufa province; today it is located in Bashkortostan.
82 Another version of this story, essentially similar in its details, is related by Marjānī, cf. *Mustafād al-akhbār*, II, 268-269; in Marjānī's version Ismāᶜīl is said to have died in 1857 in the village of Bayqibashi, (officially known as Baikybashev) in Birsk district, Ufa Province.

innovations and over-punctiliousness are not entirely absent, they nevertheless are few. Indeed one could say they don't exist and are not evident. Their dress and actions, and most of their manners and customs, conform [to the] city of Islam, Bukhara. In their feasts and banquets they do not display extravagance or characteristics that remind one of the unbelievers. They do not sit on chairs at the table, and there is no double placing of plates with forks. Women and girls never walk in the bazaar, and in fact among the mendicant women in the bazaar, Muslim women and girls are never seen. The taverns are only in the Russians' streets. /12a/ There are none among the Muslims.

The city of Semipalatinsk has two sections. In the First Section there are Russians and one *maḥalla* of Muslims. The Second Section has only Muslims and the people live among nine mosques. One is a stone mosque, seven are made of wood, and one is a small mosque without a minaret. When the *adhān* is performed and the *mu'adhdhins* sing out at the same time, the sound enchants the heart. There is only one Russian church; it is far for the Muslims and the tolling [of its bell] is not audible. It is in the *Vorstadt* suburb. One *chāqrūm's* distance from the city of Semipalatinsk is a Russian Cossack town with about a hundred houses. There is a place of worship there too. It is far away as well.

The total number of houses [in Semipalatinsk] is 1,592. Of these, 599 are in the First Section, and 993 are in the Second Section. The total number of Muslims is 3,885 males and 3,341 females. The number of [Muslim] clergy,[83] men and boys, is 23, and with their wives and daughters, 35. There are nine stone structures in the Second Section, and there are even more in the First Section. In the Second Section, the number of Kazakh households is 267, and among the Kazakhs, there are 1,461 males and 1,240 females. Among the Muslim merchants there are /12b/ 77 males and 166 females. Among the *meshchane* the number of males is 1,409 and the number

---

[83] That is, as a formally recognized group within the imperial system.

of females is 1,331. In all it is 3,698. In the environs of Semipalatinsk there are 28 factories.

In the environs of Semipalatinsk there are few Muslim villages. There are only three Muslim villages, named Āqqōltūq, Bāshkūl, and Pukūr.[84] Besides these, which have mosques, there are nomadic Kazakhs in the region. They have winter villages. These Kazakhs have great sincerity regarding religion. Most of the students and *shāgirds* studying in each of the city of Semipalatinsk's *madrasas* are Kazakhs. In their villages they always give instruction to the children and they perform their prayers communally.

218 *chāqrūms* from Semipalatinsk there is a town called Ust'-Kamenogorsk. There is also the community of a *maḥalla* there and there is a mosque. The *imām* there was Dāmullā ᶜAlī Walīd ōghlī. He studied in Qoqand, and studied the books to completion, and in Qoqand he became the chief mufti. Later, in 1865, he left Qoqand, came to Ust'-Kamenogorsk, and became the *imām*. He received his license during the time of Salīm-Girāy Muftī and Dāmullā ᶜAlī died in 1887. May the mercy of God be upon him. Amen. Indeed, he was a learned and perfect jurist. He died at age 87. After that, Mullā Yūsuf ᶜIbādallāh ōghlī Tānābāyef received a license for Ust'-Kamenogorsk and became *imām*. This Mullā Yūsuf was from among the students of Ākhūnd Mullā Aḥmad-Walī. He is a good student.

Seven hundred *chāqrūms* from Semipalatinsk there is a city called Jamanāy.[85] /13a/ There is a *maḥalla* there. There is a mosque there. A new mosque and *madrasas* were built. Walīyallāh Anwārof became *imām* there with a license. He was one of Ākhūnd Mullā Aḥmad-Walī's students. He is a

---

84 These three villages may correspond to Akkul'sk, Bashkul'sk and Pavlodar, which together with the towns of Kokpekty, and Kakaralinsk, were the only other towns in Semipalatinsk *oblast'* to officially contain mosques in the 1880's.

85 Evidently a reference to the town of Zaisan; Qurbānᶜalī identifies this figure as *imām* there until 1887/88; cf. Qurbānᶜalī Khālidī, *Tawārīkh-i khamsa-yi sharqī*, 425.

studious and intelligent person. They also have a *madrasa*. Down to the present time they are occupied with lessons.

The state of the city of Semipalatinsk and the number of its *imāms* and leaders have been described as of the year 1888. After that several left and others stayed and God knows what is hidden. Some of our sons are studying in the splendid city, [Bukhara]. May God give them useful knowledge. May they get appointed as deputies and successors, [may they] lead life in accordance with the *sharīʿa* and become suitable successors. Amen. O the Lord of the Worlds, praise be to the Lord, and God pray over Muḥammad and over his Family and all his Righteous Companions. The End.

کتاب تواریخ

سیمی پولاط قلعه

١٥

بسم الله الرحمن الرحيم

الحمد لله رب العالمين الذي فضل بعض البلدان على بعض
بالمساجد الجوامع زينت أمر الاسلام وزين المساجد
بالمنبر والمحراب والخطيب والامام وأجرى احكام الشرائع
بالآخوندين المحتسب والعلماء العظام والصلوة والسلام
على رسوله الذي شرع الصلوة بالجماعة في المساجد افضل
البقعة والمقام وعلى آله واصحابه البررة الكرام اما بعد
سنة ١٣٠٦ هجري بر منك اوچ يوز آلتونچي ايله على صاحبها افضل
الصلوات والتسليمات وسنة ١٨٨٨ ميلادي بر منك سكز يوز سكسان
سكزنچي يلده فقير الحقير بر تقصير المحتاج الى عفو ربه الغفور الرحيم
القدير المعنون بعنوان آخوند سيمبرلاط قلعه سنده ٧ يدنچي رقملي
مسجد جامع ده خطيب امام ومدرس وآخوند ملا احمد ولي السيمبولاطي
ابن علي ابن مناسب ابن اوراض محمد القزاني الاوطان ايدم اوشبو
سيمبرلاط قلعه سينك بنياد وحدث قيلنغان وقتن ثقات لاردين
مسموعم وبلدكم قدرنچه بيان قيلامن كم سيمبرلاط قلعه سي قزان
قلعه سندان [illegible] ايكي منك آلتي يوز يدي چقردم اولا مشرق
طرفنده خطاي يرينه جيكداش ويقين سيمبرلاط قلعه سي نك

وده مري

2

یری اول خطای پادشاهی نینک تصرفینده اولان قلماق و قزاق

لار ساکن بولوب اکثری کوچیلی و زیره هم قیشلاولاری دخی بولوب

نغسون سیمی پولاط قلعه سی نینک اورنینده قالماق نینک اوردالاری

بولغان علامتلاری باردور که سیمی پولاط نینک کیراسی یانینده بر

قورغان صفتی توپه پرپار شعنیدان قالماق نینک ملتوق اوقلاری

مربع کیکک اوق جدره لار تابله دور یرنی قازغانده هم سیمی پولاط

نینک اوتورغان صوقی خطای یرنده اولان آلا طاغدان چشمه لار (آلتاییدن)

جیولوب و کوپ یکک صولار قوشولوب اولوغ دریا بولوب آغادور قبله

طرفینه ایرتش کوک آسملی دریا بیک آغمی قاتی دور آستی کلا صو یول

طاشی و سوا ایرتش آسملی نینک جنوب شرقی طرفلارنده اولوغ طاغلار

باریدور پوکتای طاوی و آیرو طاوی و دوغدوغه طاوی و هم جنوب غربی

طرفینده دخی اولوغ طاولار سیمی طاو آسملی و کوکان طاوی و غیری لار

و بو طاولاردان بعض لار اسباب قالماقلار رها بالار کموشین تیکانه و ایکاک

و طباق و پیچاق و چوکان قالماق خطای نینک قلم خطی ایله مکتوب اسبابلاری

بیته بیچ علامتلار ایله سیمی پولاط نینک یری اول زمانده خطای پادشاهی

سی نینک تحت تصرفینده اولوب بعده روسیه پادشاهی ایمپراطر عسکری الوسکی

و طوبول طرف لارندان کم کم غلبه قیلیب جوروب کیلیب هیچ بر صوغوش سز

قیلمای کیلوب تصرف قیلوب قلعه و بنالار و عمارتلار قیلیب اوز خالقنی

کیتیه دن کیتوروب اوتورغان روسیه نینک خلقی اول کیلوب سیمی

پولاطقه بنا قیلغانی نینه بریونس یلدان برآز کوبراک دور اول کیلوب

2

مقام قیلغان شهر سالار بولغانلار آنلار سیمن بولاطقه عمارات لار
قیلغانده اکثری عمارتلاری آغاچدان تاش ایمادی بولغان فی الحال هم
سیمن بولاط نینک اکثر عماراتلری تاش ایماس آغاچدان آننک اوچون سیمن
بولاط نینک اطرافنده تاش ایماری اوبالاری بیک کوب بیک کوب اوّل راک زمانده
بیک یقین بولغان او یارن بیش چقرم ده آنزیاده ایماس فی الحال هم اول بیش چقرم
یردن عمارات اکثرسی آغاچ لار کیله در اوّل بنا قیلغوچی لار دان بیری عددی
طاش عمارت بولغان بشول سبیلی افواه ناسده وجه تسمیه سیمن بولاط دیوب
اسم بولغان یعنی بیری کتنه طاشن بولاط بولغان و غیرلاری کلّا آغاچ عمارات لار
اما حاضرده طاش بولاط عمارت دخی بیک کوب بولماسه ده یا ارتیق برنچه
صوقوی نینک بوینده طاو وستونده او توز تاش قلعه یری قولیق قلعه نینک
اطرافی اچ دورت چقرم یرلاندان آرتوق طوتیلیق پچانلیک و قاین لق
هم جیری قملق بولوب سبلی زراعت جلاری سیمن قلعه سندن اوتوز قرق
چقرم جه مده و آرنده بیلا غاج اسملی او غاتعلی بالالای بیک یخشی خوش
هوا جیلار تال تالیق زراعت که صالح هم ایکن لایحشی بولادو کوب وسیع
جیر اوّل زمانده سنه ۱۸۶۷ منک سکز یوز التمش ینچی یلغاچه بوش ایدی آندان صونک
دیستینه باشینه قرقتین کمش آلدادو شاهانه که فی الحال هم دخی بیک کوب
اول بیلاغاچ دیکان جیرده ایکن ایکلمای بوش جیرلارنده منکلاب جلقی هر زمن لار نینک
وهم نچه منک قوی و صغر لار او تلاب یوراتور غان یوز لاب بایلار نینک مال لاری
بولادو هر قایوسی بعضی سی نینک جلقی سی منک و بعضیسی نینک بیش یوز و بعضی سی
نینک اوچ یوز وایکی یوز ساب بوسیمن بولاط جیرینه اوّل روس خلقی کیلب

و بعد وجه تسمیه سی بولاط و یوق
یوق تلفظ طاش اولیدر ایتو لسه
نا معلوم والا ایتم وجه التسمیه
ما لنا عن البحث منه

بنا و عمارت قیلغانلار بعده قزاندان و هم آق و لادان کیلوب تورغان
مسلمانلار بوجر کیننک کوب بخشیسی و سوداخانه جای لاری توغوسیبلی
و قزاق لاری سوداغه فائده لی بولغان اوچون مسلمانلار قزاندن و اطراف
قزاندن هم آق و لادن کوچوب کیلیب سیمی پولاطنینگ سو توی ایرتیش نینگ آغمی ننگ
جوغاری جاغنه عمارت لار بنا قیلیب مقام توتغانلار سانوس خلقندان صونگ
کیلیب لارده فوقجا نیبنده دور اهل اسلام و التنگ لهذا و بو مسلمانلار نینگ اغل
کیلولارینه بر یونیر یلده ان سهل نیادد و برمس مسلمانلار قزاندان اختیار کوچوب
کیلوب هم بعضی لاری شاها آخذ متندن فیلاری سبیلی سیمی پولاطده مقام توتوب
هم قزاقیه طائفه سی برله و تاشکند شهرینه باریب سودا قیلیب کوب فراوان لیق
لاب … برمحلگه لیک مسلمانلار جمع بولغاچ نماز با جماعت ادا قیلولار اوچون
مسجد … دیو جمعیت برله اقچه جیونشوب قوم لار اول بر مسجد بنا قیلغانلار
آن مسجدینی بیک بلند قیلیب منارسی بیوک یوقاری قیلیب حاضر بو مسجد تاریخ نومر بیلی
مسجد دیب آتالادور اول وقت ده سیمی پولاطده معتبر اغنیالاردان بولغان اول
جمله سندن شیخ بای بو مسجد آتالغاشیغی مسجد دیب یعنی شیخ آغای
ترددی قیلیب اقچه جیوب صالدورغان هم آقچه نینگ کوب راغینی اوزی بیرگان
اوچون هم بو شیخ بای قزاندن پیرینده مزار باشی دیکان اولمان آتلی تو…
آوول خلق نینگ شیخی ایشم او… هم شول وقت ده سیمی پولاطلارنی یقولبا…
دیکان کوب غیرت لی … بولغان ایدی بو مسجدینه امام قیلغانلار بخارای شریفده
علم ظاهر دن تحصیل قیلیب فی الجمله قیلغان هم علم حال دان جاناغای خلیفه حسین علیه الرحمه

قزاق … اولارده اول وقتده … بولغان
… ساده و ابای … سوداگرلاری
سیبلی … قطا …
… لیک …
… الغانلار …

استقامت ایلدیلر اول ذات شریفدن مرخص احمد ایشان حضرتلری
بو احمد ایشاننڭ حضرت محمد اوغلی محمد عبد الرزاق اوغلی عبد الرزاق ایشمحمد
اوغلی ایشمحمد تیمیر اوغلی اصلی قزان نواحیسنده کتری ناچ آیلی بر مجهول
قریه دن احمد ایشاننڭ آتاسی محمد نوغمش قزانده بشنجی مسجد هم زنکار
مسجدنی بنا ایتسنده ائمه لاردن مقدم موقتا بر نیچه زمان امام
بولوب ینکا بستهده اقامت ایدوب وفات بولغان قزانلی محمد ملا دیو ملقب
ایکان ایشاننڭ آتاسی روس مملکتنده ابتدا طبع قرآن وکتاب
احداث ایدن عبد العزیز طوقطامش بن بوراش قزانی جوطای
عبد العزیز دیو معروف آدم دور بعده بو احمد ایشان بر آز ییللار امام
بولوب تورغچ شغل بای وساتولبای وغیریلار ایله بر امور دنیا احکام
شرعیده مسائللار واقع بولوب بو احمد ایشان حضرتلری ایشاننڭ
توجهیده بولوب دخی علم ظاهرده بر عالم فقیه صاحب مطالعه ذاکر کیلکی
بسیلی شغل بای اوزینینک آقچهسیله انشا ایتدی هم قرنداشی مزار باشی نینک محمد یار
حضرتلرینه جاقروب آلدوغلاری بو محمدیار حضرت ایشمحمد اوغلی ایشمحمد
وایشمحمد ایکینچی بر تعمیر عثمان قرنداش بسمحمد یار حضرتلر کیلکاچ مذکور مسجد
احمد ایشانغه شریک بولوب امام بولوب تورغانده بر آز زمان بعده قوملار دخی
کوبایکاچ دخی بر محلهلیک قوم جیولغاچ بو بر نچه عمیر داغی مسجدلرکو جیروب
قلعهنینک جیت ایکینچی طرفینه ایکینچی محله قیلیب العالم مشغول منشب مسجد اوزیره
دانک اوزینه بایلار محلهسینه ایکینچی یغشی سلق قیلیب اول اوزغاق قیلیب

دوره

بر مسجد آخر آغاچدن بنا قیلغانلار ایکنچی نومیرلی مسجد بولدی بسکوچرلکان
برنچی نومرلی مسجدکه محمدیار حضرت امام بولوب محمدجان مفتی زماننده اوکاز
آلوب اوتورغان. بو محمدیار حضرت بخارای شریفده تحصیل علوم ایلاب
ختم کتب قیلغان کشی امیر سعید زماننده هم صاحبزاده ایشانلاردن
علم حالده مرخص کشی ایکان تحشیه مطالعه ده جامع کشی ایدی بو محمدیار حضرت
بخاراده تحصیل قیلیب قایتوب اوزاق اولی مزاریشنده آز توروب شوغ باکه
چاقریلاچ کیلولاری ۱۸۰۶ منکده سکز یوز آلتونچی ییلده ایکان اوغلی
ملا فضل الله ننک آیتوی بو یونچه بعده محمدیار حضرت نچه ییللار شول برنچی
نومیرلی مسجدده امام بولوب مدرسه سنده درس آیتوب توردی و اوغلی
ملا فضل الله بخارای شریفکه تحصیل ایلاب قایتوب بعده اوزی ایشاننگ
اوغلی ملا فضل الله امام بولدی شول برنچی مسجدده بو ملا فضل الله امام
زماننده هم تدریس لیک قیلغان یوق مدرسه ده خلفه لار معلم الصبیان لار تعلیم
ایدوب تورار ایدیلار بعده ملا فضل الله نچه ییللار امام بولوب توروب بعده.
آننگ اوغلی محمد علیم مخدوم قزان نواحیسنده اولان قشقار دیر یاکی قریه ده :
دا ملا اسماعیل مدرس حضرتدن برابر تحصیل قیلوب قایتوب اوچ دورت ییل
اوکاز آلوب امام بولوب توردی بعده قوم لاری آنی یا ایتماگی عزل قیلوب ۱۸۸۲
بر مینگ سکز یوز سکسان ایکنچی ییلده اصلی سیمپولاطده تولدی باقی ملا :
یهوده ابو بکر اوغلی ملا عثمان قاری ایله بو کشی امام بولدی بو ملا یهوده بخاراده
تحصیل قیلیب حکمة العین اوقویوب کان وقتنده وظیفه جمعت ایدوب سیمی پولاطده

امیر سعید بخارا پادشاهی ایکان
عالم فقیه ... فقه کلام علم ...
... کمالات العلم لارینده ... درس ...

صاحبزاده حضرت بخارای شریف ننک مشهور مشایخ کاملاریندن ایدی فخر الحال هم اوزینده اولدی لارندان ایشان بار منه

وچواجی ... دوکاننی ابولوب بسنو داغر بو یوروب بعده شوق بر یخری نوزاری مسجد
سکنی ایکنچی بنانی اوکانی آلوب امام بولدی الحال سیمی بولاط ننک بریخنی مسجدی
ننک امامی ملا یهوده اسمی دورلعه قاری عثمان ابوبکر اوغلی ابن شفی بای وبو بر یخری نوبر
مسجد بنا قیلنغاندن بویاق توت امام بولدی اول محمد حضرت ایکنچی آننا اوغلی
ملا فضل الله اوچونچی آننا اوغلی محمد علیم توتونچی ملا یهوده عثمان قاری
دیدکی وهم بو مسجد بنا سندن بو یاقلی آلتی موذن اولدی اول شیر موذن ایکنچی رحمة الله
موذن اوچونچی سید اش موذن ابن ~~محمد یار حضرت آلتینچی احمد شاه موذن ابن~~
سید علی موذن تورتونچی سید علی موذن ابن سید شاه مذکور بشنچی حسن موذن ابن
محمد یار حضرت آلتینچی احمد شاه موذن ابن سید علی موذن فی الحال توحسن ایله احمد شاه
سلامت لا موذن دورلار ـ وهم شفی بای وسایقوللبای محله سنده یکنچی نچی راق
آغاچ مسجد بنا قیلب احمد شاه حضرت شوال ایکنچی نومیرلی مسجد ده امام بولوب توردی
کوب ییللار بعده احمد شاه قاطار لعاج آننا اوغلی ابراهیم مخدوم بخاراغه باروب
بر آز توروب شوال ابراهیم مخدوم بخاره شهرنده ایکی اوچ ییل استقامت قیلب
قایتوب احمد شاه اولنیب اوکاننی آلوب امام بولدی وبنچه ییلدان صونک دخی آخوندلیق
درجه سینه امتحان عملی الا آخوندی سیمی بولاتننک روسیه روسالاری ننک قیلتوی برلر
آخوند دیو تسمیه اولنوب جو دی ـ بعده بو ابراهیم احمد اوغلی ننک برقزنی نکاح للوب
آلدی قزان شهرندان کیلیب ملا عبید الله دامللا عبد الغیض اوغلی بسرخ آماد بولغی
سیبلی ابراهیم آخوند ایسا ننده ملا عبید الله مذکور موذن وهم معین امام
بولوب امتحان قیلنب اوکاننی آلدی ... ابراهیم آخوند وفات تیندین صونک
یانکادان

5

یانکادان امام الیوق غه بریغا واجیوب توران ایکینجی توکمیر الطاتش مسجدینه

امام بولدی حاضر امام شولدور وشغی بای صالغان ایکینجی توکمیر الی تاج

مسجد ۱۲۴۰ نجی منک سکسن یوز قریق بنجی یللار یته می دورت قصاننی برله معدوم

اولدی بعده حمد ابراهیم حضرت قشقاقریه سی نینگ مشهور بای موسی بای مرحوم

دان صدرایب دلالتی برله موسی بای کلعتور منک صوم باقر حسابیله آقچه بیروب

طاتش مسجد بنا قیلمق بولوب بالله الملانب اجل اوتومنک صوم وفا قیلمای

یتمای هم موسی بای مذکور ایکینجی کره آرتوق آقچه بیرماکاچ سیمی پولاطده

شول وقتده بر ظالم بریلاج اسمیلی بولیته میستر بولوب واتی دوختر

ایله برکیب باشلانغان مسجد حالا قالماسو قلعه نینگ نیاستی وکرنتی نه

کلیل بیرده دور دنیا دیو مقصودنی اویلاب مذکور ظالم پالیته میستر شول

وقتده غی هر قایو بایلاردن قورقیب وبعضی سین اویالتب قهرا وجبرا

آلغان شیکللی هر قایو سینه بعضیسینه برمنک وبعضیسینه اوچ منک صوم

برسون دیب خواه ناخواه تاتوب آلغان شیکللی قیلیب بجوب قاغز قارم

بیرکان آقچه نی بایلاردن جیوب شول باشلانغان طاتش مسجد تمام قیلماق

اوچون سیمی پولاط بایلاری ننگ همه سی بجوب بیرکانلاری سار روس ننگ جبر وقهر

وضرر ایرشترو ندان قورقیب شول بیرکان آقچه لار برله ایکینجی توکمیرده طاتش مسجد

صالندی دیبو نقل ایمی پولاطننگ بعض رونغلی مام لاری ایتادور

ایدیلار سکه برمزین خوب عالی بنا طاتش مسجد بنیاد قیلندی هم یاننده

مکتب بارطاتشدان صالنغان ایکی بعلمه ۱۲۶۰ نجی یلده منک سکسن یوز

بو طرح بعضی بایلاردن قاغاز ...
دیبو بعض بایلاری ... ایدی
مسموع اولمقلیدی
منه

سنه ایکنچی یلده سیمبیرسک ولایتنده تنسولوق محله ده ساکن محمد
صدیق بای ابن محمد صادق بای ابن رفیق بای اوز آقچه سی ایله عمارت قیلدی
وتعلیم الاطفال قیلدیلار ثانیاً دورت سیمبیر ولایتنک ایکنچی نومرلی مسجدنده بنا
قیلنغاندان بو یاقا حاضرغاچه امام دور اول احمد ثانی حضرت ایکنچی ابراهیم
آخوند اوچونچی ملا عبید الله ابن ملا عبد الفیض در حالا بو دور و بو مسجد
بنا سندن بو یاقا مؤذن آلتی مؤذن بولدی اول [illegible] ایکنچی سیف الدین
مؤذن اوچونچی ولی الله مؤذن دورتنچی اسماعیل مؤذن ابن احمد ثانی بشنچی
جلال الدین مؤذن ابن اسماعیل مؤذن آلتنچی شاهی مردا مؤذن بو کیسی
الحال سلامت در بعده هر اطرافدان قزاندن و اطرافندن اهل اسلام کوچوب
کیلدیلار بعضی اختیارلار و بعضی فراریلار تبدیل اسامی ایله کیلوب
سیمبیر ولایتنده مقام توتب دخی هر محلهده بر مسجدلیک قوملار جیوب اوچونچی نومر
آتامچ ضور مسجد اولوغ منکار قریه سینک [illegible] اکبر طاهر و اونسی ابراهیم
عبد اللطیف اوغللاری اوز آقچه لاری برله بنا قیلدیلار بو طاهر بو طا
طاهر دیو ملقب دور خوب بخشی سخی آدم ایدی وجه لقب شول که بو طا
طاهرنینک آغاسی بولغان حمید اسملی بو حمید [illegible] کونده بیک ضور اولوغ
سلطنت کشیسی ایکی قزاق اچنده بولدیلار سود اقیلیب [illegible] کانلار قزاق
خلق کشیسی نینک اسمن بعزه جم لقب قویدیلار بیک هوس خلق دیر شول
حمیدنی اولوغ تورالی بولغان اوچون انکا لقب بیرسه کانلار توریه حمید دیوب
آنونسی طاهرغه لقب بیرسه کانلار بو طاهر دیو یعنی کاسه توییه نینک بالاسی بو طاهر

دوبو ایدی

6

و بو اوچونچی مسجد بناسی ۱۸۳۷ نچی منک سکیز یوز اوتوز یتینچی ییللارده دور
و بو اوچونچی نوبیرلی مسجدکه بخارای شریفدن تحصیل قیلیب ختم کتب و ختم سلوک
قیلیب قایتغان اولوغ منکا قریه سی نینگ دامللا عیسی ابراهیم اوغلی امام بولدی هم
مدرسه سنده درس برله مشغول بولدی بو مسجد نینگ یاننده شولوق طلبه لار
صالغان اوچ بولمه لی آغاچ بنا مدرسه بار ایدی اول بنا فنا بولوب تو آغاچ
۱۸۷۱ نچی ییللارده شونینگ اورنیغه هم کم جماعتدان آقچه جیوب یوروب قاری
احمد صفا امام باعث بولوب طاشدن مدرسه صالندی الحال شول عمارت. مذکور داملا
حضرت عیسی شیخ بوب آدم تقوی صوفی ایدی وفاتی حتی عشر و سه قیرک آدم الار
عضوی وقتده آیا ایکی ایمدی منوم آنلار نی رسم با بعض فقیرلارغه حق دعا شغه
فقیرلارغه بیرنکه دیب کیتوب توخان صدقه لار آلمای قایتار ایدی بیادر ایکان و بعده
بو دامللا عیسی حضرت وفاتیدن صونک ۱۸۶۳ نچی منک سکیز یوز آلتمیش اوچینچی ییللارده
بخارادن ختم کتب قیلغان چیستای قلعه سینه یقین آولنینگ قاری احمد صفا
المحمد ملا اوغلی امام بولدی بعده اول وفات بولغاچ آنینگ برتوغمه اینیسی ملا
محمد حسین ملا المحمد اوغلی شولوق اوچونچی مسجدکه ۱۸۸۲ نچی منک سکیز یوز سکسان
ایکینچی ییلده امام بولدی الحال شول کشی ایدی اوچونچی نوبیرلی مسجدکه بنا
قیلغاندان بویاق اوچونچی امام دور. اول داملا عیسی حضرت ایکینچی قاری
احمد صفا اوچونچی ملا محمد حسین و بو مسجدکه بنا سندان بویان مؤذنلار توشکان اول
احمد مؤذن ایکینچی محمد صادق مؤذن ابن احمد اوچونچی صالح مؤذن
تورتینچی عبد الجبار مؤذن ابن صالح مؤذن الحال دسلامت و بعده دخی بیشینچی لاط

6

قلعه سی آتوب خلق کو بایب جیت یاقده دخی بر محله لیک غلو بدلعاج مسجد کبر
یراق بولدوق دیو جماعت لار جیوشوب آقچه جیوب جمع قیلب دخی تو تنچی
عمر نومرن مسجد بنا قیلدیلار آیحشی ضوبر آغاج مسجد ۱۸۴۷ سنه منک سکز یوز
قرق یدنچی یلده بو مسجدکه بخارای شریفده تحصیل قیلغان ختم کتب وختم سلوک
قیلغان عالم وفقیه وفاضل وجامع ومتدین متقی دامللا ضیاء الدین حضرتلری
امام بولدی عبد الله احمد مفتی دان امتحان بیلن بو دامللا ضیاء الدین حضرت خوب آدم
خوش صورت وخوش سیرت بر آدم ئوزال ایدی خوش مجلس وخوش خلق هم
مدرسه ده شاگردلاری کوب بولوب درس ایتوب عمر کیچورادی بو عزیز ۱۸۷۹
منک سکز یوز یتمش توقوزنچی یلده وفات بولدی رحمة الله علیه آمین بعده
آننک اوغلی … اوز وقتنده مؤذن ومعین امام بولوب تورغان قیرقاطراف … یلکان تنچی
قریه سنده یاشی وقتنده یعقوب حضرتنه برز تحصیل قیلغان ملا احمد جان بن عبد الله
اوغلی دامللا ضیاء الدین حضرت وفات تیدین صونک … اجیوب امام ایتوب قه
اوتوردی فی الحال امام شول اور … وبو تو تنچی نومر مسجد بنا سندن بو یاقی ایکنچی
امامی دوواول دامللا ضیاء الدین حضرتی اولیدو اوغلی ایکنچی ملا احمد جان ابن عبید الله وبو
تو تنچی مسجد بنا سندن بو یاق مؤذن توردو اول نعما مؤذن ماسر آقونک
شینچی بابای ایدی ایکنچی عبد الغفور مؤذن اوچونچی ملا احمد جان مؤذن تو تنچی علیم
مؤذن در … دخی بشنچی نومرلی مسجد سیمی بولدلار … ایتش صونکنک ایکنچی جان … فنده
جنوب طرفنده اول قزاق طائفه سندن جوماش اسملی بای قزاق بنا قیلغان آغاج مسجد
… سنه ۱۸۲۲ منک سکز یوز یکرمه ایکنچی یلده اول مسجدکه امام بولغان اوکان …

مزبخاری

7

بخارالرده تحصیل علوم قیلیب کیلکاچ هم سمی‌پلاتنسکده توروب تمام آیلاب ختم کتب
قیلغان کورکار چین آقسقالی ملا عبد الکریم ابو بکر اوغلی اول ملا عبد الکریم نینک
خلقی قزاق اندرینه یرنشمی و اول اوزی ده قزاق لرده اتمامی آنده برایکی یل
تورماغ اوزینی عمل قیلیب بعده اول مسجد نینک شرکی بیشتا طائفه سندن پچکا
ده مشهور ملا عبد الله مدرسه دن برآز تحصیل قیلغان هم آدای حضرتدن
قرائت اوکانگان ملا محمد امین منصوف امام بولدی بعده اول مسجد نینک
قامی بولوب اسکی کاج چریکاج آننک اورنینه قوم لاری بالالری آقچه جیوب جمعیت اوزره
۱۸۷۶ منک سکز یوز یتمش آلتونجی یلده بر تحشی اولوغ آغاچ مسجد بنا قیلدیلار بو
مسجد نینک بانیسی سندن بولوق امام فی الحال هم شو ملا محمد امین دور و هم مسجد نینک یاننده
اوچ بولملی آغاچ مدرسه بنا قیلدیلار شول تعلق محله ده توروچی قزاق طائفه سندان
بو تعویچی مدرس العلما صاحب الهمت تلاوت بابی آبدان اوغلی اوزاقیه سی الملک و تعلیم علوم
قیلنا دور و هم ۱۸۶۷ منک سکز یوز سکسان یدنچی یلده بو امام نه شریک قیلیب قویدیلار
اصلی اسم بوعلا کیف ملا حسام الدین ملا زین العابدین اوغلی امام الیقه شریک
معین امام المرتبه مذکور امام ملا محمد امین یوق وقتده نائب لادور و بو تیجه مسجد
ایرتش صنوقی نینک آرغی یاغنده فی الحال هم اکثری قومی قزاق خلقی اماکویس
دیمشدان هم بالالری بیشتالتی عدد کینه باو غیرلاری کلکا قزاق طائفه سندان
دور بابی تقیرلاری جمعیت بشش یوزاودان زیاده رق برقریه کلان دور
اکثری نینک خانه لاری نینک تعابالاری مسطح تره زه لاری سوراخ محض قیلنده
اما اوزلاری کرچند یکنه تعدیل ارکان بولماسه نماز باجماعت بیک جیولادلار

مذکور امام ملا محمد امین بار اوقینده
مذکور امام ملا محمد امین
بابی تعداد اودور
بیک ارتوغ منده

7

وطلبه لارى ذهن پویه كدوغی متحقق اولماى مسح بر لكنه پیشی باشی چلاب
ايناقو مسجدكه كيلالار خدا قبول قيلسون ديهم اوزلارى امام الار حسب بيك
تربيه قيلالار بو بشنجى مسجدكه بناسنده بولوب ايكى مؤذن بولدى اول مذكور
منارسز جولما مسجدى وقتنده وليد اسملى مؤذن ايدى بر يوز اون يلسغه
كيلوب وفات بولدى اوستكامينده امام بولمش ملا على نينك آتاسى ايدى ايكنجى مؤذن
عبد الله مؤذن دوردر هم اوشبو مسجدنينك محله سينه توتاش دخى صونكنده آسغى باشنده
آلتونجى توميرلى مسجد بناسنه ١٢١٣ منك سكز يوز يكرمه توقزنجى يلده بنا قيلنغانده
آغاجدن منارسز غنه. تنو بايكوكاو على باى قزاق طائفه سندن بو محله ده
هم همه سى قزاق خلقى بونينك دارحسابى بريوز ايللى باربو مسجدكه امام ملا احمد جان
آلطاى باى اوغلى قزاق طائفه سندن سيرم بولاط شهرنده آخوند ملا احمد ولى ده
تحصيل علوم قيلب سليم كراى مفتى زماننده اوفى ده امتحان قيلنب اوكازيله
امام بولدى هم مسجدنينك يانينده مكتبى تعليم اطفال حكيمه ايله مشغولدر بو مسجدنينك
بناسندان بورياق اوچ امام ادنا باجان اسملى قزاق ملاسى ايكنجى نعمتجان اسملى
اوفى آذيا زيليك ايدى اوچونجى امام ملا احمد جان ابن آلطاى باى وبانى مسجد مذكور حاضرغى
تنوباى باى كاوكانو جلجل ايدى بيك سخى باى ايدى مسافرپرور ومهمان دوست
سخى وبه يك برله مشهور هم دولتى بيك كوب ايدى آخير عمرينكاچه دولتى
توردى اوزى توقصان سكز ياشنده ١٨٨٧ منك ده سكز يوز سكسان
يدنجى يلده وفات بولدى خدا رحمت ايليه آمين وارث اوغلى قالمادى اوغلان لارى
نجه لر مدد او زنده مقدم وفات بولمشلار لكن كمير قيزى قالدى بر واسقت يا تحار ز
ايرى

8

ایری باقیزاق ابراهیم نراکان اوغلی قالغان مال اللارنی اول فاسق ابراهیم آللار ایکن

وقت وفاتنده مال آنزایدی بو ساتغ وقتینه نظر مرحوم تنوبای حاجی اوزی نینک

صحتنده خیر واحسان قیلیب صدقه قیلیب اوزینه صرف قیلدی هم اوزی نینک مسجد

یاننده تورغان عالی عمارتلار جوت جیرلارنی هم مسجد وقف قیلیب وفات بولدی

خدا قبول الیلیه امین وینه دخی سیمی بولاط قلعه سنده خلق کوبایب دخی بر محلّه

اورون بولوب ایدیجی نوبیرلی مسجد جامع آغاچدان بنیت ضعف قیلیب سنه ۱۲۱۸ منک سکز یوز

ایللی ایکنچیسی بلده جماعت داره آقچه جیوب قوم جماعت آقچه سی براه بنا قیلمدن بو

مسجد امام بولدی بخاراده تحصیل قیلغان ختم کتب قیلغان اصلی ماچکار آوقی لی نینک

ملا زین العابدین البسنداوغلی بو ملا زین العابدین اوچ تورت ییل امام بولوب تورغاچ

کسل فالج غه گرفتار بولوب امامتدن قالوب بش ییل مقداری مدت سلاادی وردی

اول وقتده بر موذن مصطفی سعید اوغلی امام بولوب اداقیلیب توردی بعده ۱۸۶۳ سنه

منک سکز یوز آلتمش اوچونجی یلده بخاراده تحصیل قیلغان اصلی اوفا او یازلیک

چاپلی قریه سینه یقین صوقایش اسملی قریه لیک ملا افضل الله نعمة الله اوغلی

امام بولدی هم بو کمسه بخاراغه بارماسدن مقدم چاپلی اوفالنده مشهور داملا ابراهیم

حضرتده اوقوغان بو ملا فضل الله سلیم گرای مفتی زماننده امتحان قیلینب اوکاز

آلغاچ سیمی بولاط قیلیب مسجد مذکورده بر جمعه نمازنده خطبه ده مرض حالنده

اوقوب بعده صاحب فراش بولوب بر ایکی آیدان صونک وفات بولدی کسل

سیل ایدی خدا رحمت ایلیه آمین ابجمع موذنینک وفاتندان صونک بو ایدیجی

مسجد نینک قوم لاری بخارای شریف دن بر فقیر مؤلف هذا تاریخ نی چاقردیلار

[illegible]

امام اولوب اوچون قایتوب نکره دیتوقهم. بنوم شول وقت یلده بخارای شریفده اون
ایکی یل استقامت قیلوب ختم کتب قیلانمه ییتکا وقتمز ایدی اول سیمیج بعد الله داملا
ضیاء الدین حضرتنده عقایدنی اوقوب یکی ارغه باروب دخی عقاید الحق
بولوب استاذمز درس علم کلامده داملا نجم الدین علیه الرحمة ایدی شول ایلنده ختم کتب
قیلدوق هم مسئلهده رسنده استاذمز داملا نیاز بلخی علیه الرحمة ایدی هم حضرت کلان صاحبزاده
حضرتنک اوغلی حضرت میان فاروق علیه الرحمة‌گه دست انابت قیلماق ایله وبو
استاذ عزیزلاردن رخصت آلوب قایتوب شول یلدا دار الامتحان اوفی قلعه سینه
بارب سلیم گرای مفتی زماننده امتحان قیلنوب مقبول اولوب صاحب امتحان ممیزلار
اولارنی سز آخوندلیققه لایق ایکانسز دیو آخوندلیق ومدرسلک وخطیب
وامام دیو امتحان نامه بیردیلار بس شول امتحان نامه ایله وقوم لارنینک رجعا لاری ایله
سنه ١٨٦٢ منک سکز یوز آلتمش ایکنچی یلده مذکور ییدنچی نومرلی مسجد جامعغه
اوکاز آلوب مدرس وخطیب واخوند اولدوم بن فقیر ملا احمد ولی ابن عملی ابن
ملا سنب ابن اورفی محمد الله وداری - هم بو مسجدنک یاننده شول یلده آچماچه
عمارت قیلنوب اوچ مدرسه بار ایدی آنده یخه للار شاکردلار جمعیت لیک
اوز زمانه بقدر حال درس گوی لیک برله مشغول اولوب تورامز وهم سنه ١٨٦٤ منک
سکز یوز آلتمش تورتنجی یلده دخی مدرسه گرک ابو العاج شول آماچ مدرسه یانینه
ایکی بولمه لی طاشدان بینا ییتمشی عالی مدرسه بنا قیلدوردی مرحوم محمد واصل حاجی
بای مرتضی اوغلی خواجه سیدف وصیتی قیلغانی آقچه سی برله اول محمد واصل حاجی
نینک اوغلی محمد یوسف نه محمد مصطفی بای خدا تعالی قبول ایلیه آمین فی الحال

شول

شوال مدرسلارده شاکردلار یاتاق کوب جیوب تدریس لیکده مشغول ایمز
وبو ایکنچی نومیرلی مسجدنینک بنا سنیدان باقی بو اوچ امام بولدی اوّل الاّ زین العابدین
ایکنچی ملا فضل الله اوچونچی ملا احمد ولی آخوند موافق هذا التاریخ فی الحال کمینه
دور تشکراً الحمد لله رب العالمین — وبو ایکنچی مسجدده بنا سنیدان بو وقت اوچ مؤذن
اوّل ثابت ملا مؤذن ایکنچی مصطفی مؤذن اوچونچی محمد جان مؤذن ابن مصطفی
مؤذن الحال بودور و دخی هر یرده جماعت کیلیب سیمی پولاطده مقام توتولاری سببلی
دخی بر مسجد لیکن قوم آغاچ بنا قیلدوردی سنه ۱۲۸۱ منک ایکی یوز ایللی توقوزنچی
یللارده بر مسجد آغاچدان سکزنچی نومرلی مسجد عتیت الله اسمیلی بو مسجدده امام بولدی
قربان نواحینده قازان ایلی اسمیلی قریه نینک ملا حسام الدین قرآن آلدی افندی اوّل الاّ
برار اوقوغان نخشی قاری ایدی خوش خلق بو ملا حسام الدین نینک لقبی سیمی پولاطده
پیشی ملا دیلار ایدی و بو کیشی نچه یللار امام بولوب توروب و قاری ایتاچ میت آ
طائفه سیدان بخارای شریفده تحصیل علوم قیلیب ختم کتب و ختم سلوک قیلغان
ملا عبد الجبار رحمه الله اوغلی اتفاقا بخارادن قایتوشنده سیمی پولاط تعلّق
قایتماق بولوب هم سیمی پولاطده قایتوب توروب مذکور ملا حسام الدین نینک
قزینه تزوّج قیلیب آلیب نچه یللار مدرسده تعلیم قیلیب توروب هم دین امام بولوب
اوکان الوب بعده ملا حسام الدین وفات بولغاچ ملا عبد الجبار امام بولوب
وخطیب و مدرّس بولدی بو مسجدنینک یانیده مدرسه سی بار هم ملا عبد الجبار زمانینده
یخشی درس توزیلیک قیلیب توردی بعده اوّل ملا عبد الجبار سفر حج غه کیتوب سنه ۱۲۸۱
منک ایکی یوز [illegible] یلیده قایتوب کیلکانده طوغرسیاده کرنتین

9ب

یاتقان یرده بحکم الٰهی وفات بولدی اندان یاوق بو سلر نچه نعمرلی مسجدده مؤذن دهم
کیمسه شاکردلار امام بولوب توردیلار شیرکه ملا عبد الجبار نینک مرحوم نینک اوغلی
بار ایدی بخارای شریفده تحصیل علوم قیلب یاتقان ششه‌لی بودر تا امام قیلامز
دیب قوم لاری سکز یل کوتدیلار هم کیمسه نی امام قیلاتوروب و بو مخدوم ابن
ملا عبد الجبار ملا اصلاح الدین بخارادن قایتمادی قایتمام دیب قوم لارینه براکی
یل کوتدوروب بعده اخلاص العوام معلوم مصدر اقنجه هر تورلی سوزلر ایشتکان
بولوب چار مخدوم مذکور یرلده قایتوب کیله یاتساده بر طالب جاه امام
بولور اوچون بیک تماده آرزوده بولوب تورغان واده بوجخر مسجد نینک اقامه
شریک بولام دیب قوم لارینه تورلی فتنه و جنجال و بر یر سینه غداوتلار ینه
سبب بولغان و مسجد مذکور نینک امامنه بیک خوا قیلغان اصلی تومانلیک ملا عبد الحق ابن ملا
اسملی کمسنه‌نی امام قیلدیلار فی الحال شول دور امام و بو سلر نچه مسجد نینک باسندن
بو یاق املام اوچ اول ملا حسام الدین ایکنچی ملا عبید الجبار اوچونچی ملا عبد الحق
ابن ملا عماد الدین دور و بو مسجد نینک باسندن بو یاق مؤذن بردر رحیم الله
مؤذن ابن سید اش مؤذن فی الحال شول صفی الله دور وهم دخی خلق جماعت
کوبایکاچ دخی بر تورت نچی مسجد بنا قیلدیلر اونبش آقچه سی برلان اصلی طاشکند
کیچواقلی نینک محمد حاجی حاجی اسماعیل اوغلی ایشتر کوی ۱۸۶۲ منه سکز
یوز سکسان ایکنچی ییلده بو مسجدکه امام بولدی ملا کمال الدین محمد رحیم اوغلی
اصلی قرآن طرفندن دور اول قشقاریده اوقوغان بعده بخارا ده اوچ
یل توروب تحصیل قیلغان و بو مسجدده مؤذن عبید مؤذن دور وهم یانده

مدرس ...

تحصیل علوم قیلدی و توراوچ
دو ... طرفنده ...
تعویم یل اسلام بولدی ...
منه

٥١

مدرسه سی بابر بعد الحال تعلیم ایله مشغول در و شاکردلاری بیش دهه او
صورانیه نه تابع میتر یحکی کی کیلب تعمیر تورغان مسجدینی لار طرده تورر
عدد دو بیرسه طاشتی و غیرالاری باجه سه قالدی آغاچیدان در کلسنده
بوتون بیش وقت و جمعه نماز اهم او قولادور قدیم کوب بولادور بیرقایده سنده و بو
مسجدلارده امام لاری بر عدد دو شریکای ایاسلاری مکر بعضی مؤذن نینک
اوکا تینه معین امام دیتو یا ریلمان بار و بو مسجدلار دان باشقه ذخیره سیمی بولا
ایکی مسجد جماعت لار مسجدی دیب آتالادور بیرسه سیمی پولاطنینک اول باشلیغان
زمانینده تاشکنددان صاحب لار کیلب سیمی پولاطده مقام توتقانلار قزاقیه
طائفه سندن قوچقاتون آلوب سیمیده تورغوب قالغانلار تاشکنده قایتمای
شول پیتا قیلغانلار ماسزبرلیک مسجد تاشکند مسجدلاری نینک فصادی و زروشی
ایله بو مسجد عوام خلقی توقال مسجدی دیب تسمیه لارماسه بولغان اوچون
دور بو مسجد نینک بنا سنه او شبوته ۱۸۸۱ نچی مینگ سکز یوز سکسان بیرنچی یلده تو قصان
یلغه قریب بولکه اکه بوتوقال مسجد امام صاحب طائفه سندن جالاقزاق اسم
لنمش ملا محمد نیاز اسمی کسنه امام او کازسز اوزلاری نینک قولداری نینک
خواتش و تلاوتلاری ایله امام بولوب تعمیرادور سیمی پولاطده آخوند ملا احمد
دن تحصیل قیلغان شخص متدین دور و هم صاحب لار نینک ایکنجی مسجد بنا
قیلغان اوزاقچه سیر ایله سیمی پولاطده یوطراریله مقام توتوب قالغوچی اصلی
تاشکندلیک میر قربان بای آقونتبای اوغلی دیومر قربان بای نینک لقبی دکاش
اید بو مسجد هم بیشی الوغ ایکی مناره بادر بو یاقولی مسجد آغاچدن بو مسجدده امام صاحب

چالاقزاق لار علمدن دیب هم
اشتغال ایدورلر علیهم

طائفه سنده ملا احمد جان قاری ابن ملا مسلم ابن مؤمن جان بابای بو قاری احمد جان سیچی بولا طلبه
مدرسه آخوند ملا احمد ولی ده قاری و حافظ کلام الله بولوب بر آز تحصیل علوم قیلب
منذ نوری مسجده امام بولمشدر و بو ایکی مسجد نینک یاننده مدرسه لاری و مکتب یوق بو صبیانلار
لارنینک صبیان بالالاری هر قایو مدرسه‌گه باروب اوقیلار و بو ایکی مسجد جماعه‌سی دو جاودی بای
صونکرانیه دن میتریجکی‌نینک کاه بیرلماید و سیچی بولالار ننک و یازندان فاو طلبه‌نی کناکه
بیرلوب تو عام و وفات و نکاح لارنی شونکا ریازلار یازاسی لاری کیلیه قوم لاری حج
تاشکند لیکو و قزاق حکمنده دور کلی حال صالدات بیرمای جهانکارق آقچه سی دیتو بیرالار
توتون بیلی اول زمانده ارق بعمارت چالا قزاق لار بیک غنی بای لاری توب
ایدی فی الحال عمه سی فقیر اولمشدر و اکثر غنی بی نهایه بولغان بای بالالاری ننک بعضی
اوروصیه کوچ و بعضی سی گدای اولدلار غنی وقت لرینده هم حضلت لاری ایرته
نمازینه توزمای قریب بیشین کاچه تره نره لارنی یاپیب قیلیلدر ایدی الحال هم جانی
کونلارنینه ساعت اون برگاچه یاتالار غفلت دندور بو ایسه بس سیچی
بولا شهرنده جمع مسجد جامع اون بردور ایکی صونکنک آرغی غمنده و ایکی صاتیار
لار مسجدی و بیدینه نیبار سی طاش دور و غیری لاری آغاچدان دور و بارچه
سنده بش وقت جمعه اوقولادور و عید نمازی هم بعض یلده هر قایوسیده
اوقولادور و بعض یلده جیو شوب لماش مسجد نینک یاننده احاطه قیلنغان وسیع
یرنیا شونده جیولوب اوقیلار اگر چند یکه صحراده وضع قیلغان موافق سنت
مصلی بولماسا ده بر توتار جیو لیش دیب باریلار فقیر اوز مسجدده قوم کثیر برله
اوقومر و غیری لاری هم بعضلاری اوز مسجدلرینده اوقیلار و بو مسجدلارننک

رهی

11

ایرا باشقه منه

هم قایوسی روسیه اهالی برله آرالاشوب اولتورغان ایاس صونکنده بوداق غیرابغنده
مسلمان قوملاری نینک اوی یللاری باچه سی روسیه جماعه سندن ایرا باشقه بولاب
اولتورغانلار کوچه لاری دیگر توتون لاری توتونکه آرالاشمایدور مگر کیم ملا
عبد الحق امام ابو الغازی عتیبه مسجدی دیب آطاللادور سکزنچی نومرلی مسجد قوملاری
نینک توتون لاری روسیه توتونینه آرالاشه دور دخی مسجد بولدی ده قایو
در کیم مذکور مسجدلرنی اول آقچه سی برله صالغان بای نینک مسجدی نینک اول بای
اسمی ایله بولادر مثلا اوچونچی مسجد بوطا مسجدی ینه طاهر بای وطالقبلی
کمسنه صالغان سکزنچی نومرلی مسجد عتیبه مسجدی دیلدر وتوقزنچی نومرلی
مسجد ایشتراکو مسجدی دیلدر وغیری لاری جمعیت آقچه سی ایله بنا قیلنغان
مسجد امام لاری اسمی ایله آطایورلار مثلا رضا حضرت مسجدی ومحمد یار حضرت
مسجدی وملا احمد ولی آخوند مسجدی وهکذا :: الحمد لله حمد الشاکرین سیمیبولاط
شهرنده مکتوب هر مسجدده سلطه وعما برله جماعت ده جماعت کوب خصوصا
جمعه نمازنده بیک کوب بولادور — وهم مذکور صارت مسجد نینک دوقش مسجد
یانده حفظ قیلنب موضع خاصده مذکور حفظ قاش نینک اوی نینک خاص بولمه
سنده محفوظ تربیه لار برله قویلغان ومذکور خانه سینک اچنده بر بولمه خاصده
محفوظ موی مبارک آنحضرت صلی الله علیه وسلم بار والشکر علی هذا کمال الشکر
بر عزیز شیخ ایشان توکنکان صاحب نفس وصاحب کرامت اسلامبولده نسغرج
دان قایتوب کیلوشنده سلطان عبد المجیددن آلغان سلطان نینک آتا سینه وقت
مرضنده مرضندن شفا تابوقینه سبب بولوب مذکور والده سلطان عبد المجید بو

ایشانغه دنیا مالندان انواع جواهر وطلا بریسه ده طلب وقبول قیلمای دوی مبارك
خزینه خانه‌دان برادانه بیرلسه ایکان دیو طلب قیلیب آلوب ایکی دانه مبارك آلوب
کیلوب سیمی بولاطه مدکور بوقاش بایعه بیروب کیتکان ادزی دخی سفر حجغه کیتوب
متوجه بولوب بارشنده جولده وفات بولغان مسلمان آوللنده ایکی مسجدلی جوق
کیلدیکلی قریه ده ابهت برلر قران آرسنده فی الحال اول زیارتگاه بولوب بعض
اثرلاری بارلمش وقبرلرننك اوچینه بر [illegible] سنبر یاشل آغاج اوسکان باشش
دیلار ~~مسافرلارننك نقلی~~ هیچ ولدینده اول طریقه آغاچ نی کورکانم یوق
دیلار مسافرلارننك نقلی بر غریب عجیب همیشه قیش وجای ده جوغی دائی یاشیل
نسبز بولوب تورغان اغاچ دیلار [illegible] الحمدلله سیمی بولاطه ده شرافت لاباد
کثرة مساجد واهل اسلام ووجود موی مبارك نبینا محمد صلی الله علیه وسلم
واهلی دخی تواضع لی خلق لار تکبر صفت لاری یوق ومعیشت لاررنده دخی
بدعت وتکلف وخلاف شرع بالکلیة منتفع بولماسه ده هر نه آزراق درس
قلیل کالعدم اقتضاسنچه ظاهرا کوریلدی دور هر نه قدر حال البانس وحرکت لاری
ورسم رسوم لاری اکثری موافیق شهر اسلام بخارا مانند طوی وضیافت لارده
تکلف که مفضی اسراف اولان فعل لار وتشبه کفار بولغان حصلت لار یوق
اوستال دستورخانده [illegible] لارینه اوتوزنچا [illegible] لار وتیرلکه لاری
ایکنترلابان قیماق لاری یوق وبازارده نساء جماعه سی قز وخاتون
اصلا یورماس حتی گدای خاتون لاردان بازارده مسلمان اهلندان قز
وخاتون اصلا کورونمایدور روس خانه قباق لاری هم روسیه کوچه لرنده کنه

مسلمان

12

مسلمانلرنینك یوق وسیمی پولاط شهری اوزنده ایکی چاسن اولوب بیروای
چاسده روسیه لر طائفه سی دورهم بجمله مسلمانلر دخی آنده - وافتروی
چاسده کُلاّ مسلمان طائفه سی اولوب توقز مسجدلری سنده اوتوز میش خلق لری
بر طاش مسجد ویدیسی آغاچ مسجد وبرمنارسز کچک مسجد هم آذان ایتکان
وقتده مؤذنلر بر وقتده ایتکانده کورولداب آذان طاوشی ایله
قلبکه فرح بخش ایترلر حاصل اولادو روسیه ننك چیرکاوی فقط بر
اولهم مسلمانلرغه یراق طاوشی ایشتولماید و روفرشتات دیدورسیمی
پولاط قلعه سندن برچقروم فاصیله ایله صالنمش قزاق اوروصقالدسی بریونه
اوی متدارلر آقیل آنده هم معبدلری بارول هم یراق وجمیع اویلار حسابی برمنك
بش یوز توقصان ایکی - ١٥٩٢ - بولوب بوننك بش یوز توقصان توقزی
٥٩٩ - بیروای چاسده روسیه لر وبوننك توقز یوز توقصان اوچی - ٩٩٣ -
افتروی چاسده بولوب مسلمانلر جمع نفوسی جانی ایا سیر ایرکاکلر ٣٨٨٥ -
اوچ منك سکز یوز سکسان بش واوناچیلاری - ٣٣٤١ - اوچ منك اوچ
یوز قرق بر دوروودچاونای لار نفوسی ایرکاکلری باللاری برنه یکرمه اوچ
٢٣ - اوناچیلار قیزلاری برله اوتوزبش - ٥٣ - دوروواوی لارننك
افتروی چاسده توقز عدد طاش پولاطبار وبیروای چاسده طاش پولاط کورك
وافتروی چاسده اوی برله توبکان قزاق طائفه سیننك اوی لارنك عددی
٢٦٧ - ایکی یوز آلتمیش یدی وقزاقلار نفوسی ایرکاکلاری - ١٤٦١ - برمنك
توقز یوز آلتمش براوناچلاری ١٢٤٠ - برمنك ایکی یوز قرق کوب مسلمانلار نفوسی

١٢٢-

٧٧- یتمش یدی ییرکانلاری - واو تاریخی لاری ١١٦٦ - بر یوز آلتمش آلتی
دوشمیشنچی نغوس لاری ایرکاکی لاری ١٢٠٥٩ - بر منک توقز یوز توقز داوتاریخی
لاری - ١٣٠١٣ - بر منک اوچ یوز اوتوز بردور جمعسی ٣٦٩٥ - اوچ منک آلتی یوز
توقصان سکز . دُرت اطرافنده بولاطله ١٢٨ یوز بکرمی سکز مشابوط لاریا رسیمیبولاط
تابعه سی نینک اطرافنده مسلمان اول لاری آز آق قولتوق - وباشقا ول -
ویکرمی سیملی اوچ قریه مسلمان اولیغنه بار مسجدلی ومؤذن غیری لاری اطرافنده
کوچمه لی خلق قزاقیه طائفه سی دور قیشلاولی آویل لار بار اول قزاقیه
طائفه لاری یخشی دینکا اخلاصلی لاری بار سمی پولاط شهری نینک هر مدرسه سنده
طالب شاکردلاری اکثری قزاق طائفه سندان اوقوب ترالار هم اوز آویل لارنده
همیشه تعلیم صبیان ایدوب نماز جماعت قیلیب تورالار وهم سمی پولاط ده ایکی
یوز اون توقز چقروم یرده اوستکامین گورسکی دیکان قلعه بار آنده هم بر محله
قوم دور مسجد بار آنده امام داملا علی ولید اوغلی ایدی خوقندده مفتی ترداربولوب
توشان بعده ل ١٢٨١ منک سکز یوز آلتمش نچی یل لارده خوقندان کیلکاچ
شول اوستکامین ده امام بولدی سلیم گرای مفتی زمانده اوکاز آلوب واول
داملا علی ١٢٨٧ منک سکز یوز سکسان یدنچی یلده وفات بولدی خدا رحمت ایلیه آمین
خوب آدم فاضل وکامیل فقیه ایدی سکسان توغز یاشنده وفات بولدی . بعده
اوستکامین ده اوکاز آلوب امام بولدی ملا یوسف عبدالله اوغلی تاتار بایوق
بو ملا یوسف آخوند ملا احمد ولی تلمیذی جمله سندن دور یخشی مطالعه دار در
وهم سمی پولاط قلعه سندان یدی یوز چقروم یرده جمنای اسملی شهر بار
آنده .

تحصیل قیلیب ختم کتب قیلغان هم خوقندده

آنده دخی بر محلّه ده مسجد بار آنده یانکا مسجد و مدرسه لار بنا قیلنب انده امام بولدی اوشانداق
برله ملّا ولی الله انواری بوهم آخوند ملّا احمد ولی تلمیذی جمله سندان دور
نجیب مطالعه دار و صاحب فطانت شخص دور بونلارنینک هم مدرسه لری
بار بعد رحال درس برله مشغول لار دور سمی پولاط شهری نینک بو
احوالی امام و معتمد لاری فی الحال سنه ۱۸۸۶ مینک سکز یوز سکسان التی
یلده مذکور لار دور من بعد کم لار کیتوب کم لار بولار و الله سبحانه علام
الغیوب و بعض لاریمزنینک مخدوم لاریمزدا دخی بلده فاخره ده
تحصیل علوم قیلیب تورار لار خدای علم نافع ویروب جای نشین و قائم
مقام اولوب استقامت شرع ایله متّصف بولوب خیر و ارشاد لار
اولماقلاریمزنی نصیب و روزی ایلکای ایدی

آمین یا رب العالمین والحمد لله
وصلی الله علی محمد و آله و صحبه
اجمعین
تمت تمام

Qurbānᶜalī Khālidī (1846-1913)

Qurbānᶜalī Khālidī al-Āyagūzī al-Chūchāgī is the author of several major and very substantial historical works dealing primarily with the history of eastern Kazakhstan and of northwestern Chinese Turkestan. Qurbānᶜalī's historical writings include both manuscript and printed works and his works would stand out in almost any field as substantial monuments in their own right.[86]

Qurbānᶜalī was born in 1846 in the town of Ayaguz, a Cossack and merchant settlement at that time officially known as Sergiopol', and located in eastern Kazakhstan. While officially registered as a Chala Kazakh, Qurbānᶜalī's ancestry on both his father's and his mother's sides was from the village of Urnashbash, in Kazan province's Kazan district. In a genealogical treatise Qurbānᶜalī traces his ancestry back to a figure named Türkmān Bābā, who is said to have come from Khiva during the reign of Abū'l-Ghāzī Bahādur Khan (r. 1643-1663) and to have settled in the village of Sarda, in Kazan province. In Sarda Türkmān Bābā had three sons, Bāymurād-Qōl, Muḥammad-Qādirqōl, and Bīkbāw. Bīkbāw settled in the nearby village of Urnashbash, where he had a son named ᶜUthmān (Gosman). ᶜUthmān's son was Bīkqōl and Bīkqōl's son was Khālid, Qurbānᶜalī's father. Qurbānᶜalī's mother, ᶜAfīfa, was also descended from Türkmān Bābā, but her ancestry was from Türkmān Bābā's son Muḥammad-Qādirqōl.[87]

Qurbānᶜalī's initial education was in Ayaguz in the *madrasa* of Shaykhalislām Ākhūnd b. Muḥammad-Ṣādiq b. Ismāᶜīl (d. 1889).[88] Later he studied in Semipalatinsk, in the *madrasas* of the Seventh and Eighth Mosques. He identifies a certain Mullā Mālik Afandī as one of his teachers, and as his main source for his history of Semipalatinsk; we know from this history that Mullā Mālik served briefly as *imām* of the Seventh Mosque,

---

86 On Qurbānᶜalī cf. Mirqasïym Gosmanov, *Qaurïy qaläm ezennän*, 2nd ed., (Kazan, 1994), 317-322; D. Kh. Karmysheva, "Kazakhstanskii istorik-kraeved i etnograf Kurbangali Khalidi," *Sovetskaia Etnografiia* 1971 (1), 100-110.

87 This genealogy is located in a manuscript in the private collection of M. A. Usmanov; cf. Gosmanov, *Qaurïy qaläm ezennän*, 323.

88 Karmysheva, "Kurbangali Khalidi," 101.

and presumably taught in the *madrasa* as well. Qurbānᶜalī also studied in the Eighth Mosque under a certain ᶜAbdaljabbār, who originally came from Chistopol' district in Kazan Province.[89] We also know from the manuscripts in our publication that ᶜAbdaljabbār had studied in Bukhara. While in Semipalatinsk Qurbānᶜalī earned the rank of *qārī*.[90]

By 1874 Qurbānᶜalī had completed his studies and was appointed *imām* of the Tatar mosque in the frontier town of Chuguchak, a commercial center and garrison town located just inside Chinese territory, but still within the Kazakh steppe. Here he fulfilled the duties of *imām*, but also taught in the local Tatar *madrasa*. He would retain this post until his death in 1913, and all of his historical works were written in Chuguchak. In 1881 he became the Chief *qāḍī* for the local Tatars, Kazakhs, Sarts, and Uyghurs; that is, for the entire Muslim community save the Dungans, that is, the Hui, or ethnic Chinese, Muslims.[91]

Qurbānᶜalī's earliest work is entitled *Tārīkh-i jarīda-yi jadīda*. It exists in several manuscript copies, but was also published in Kazan in 1889. The work is essentially an account of a pilgrimage he undertook in 1885 from Chuguchak to the town of Kuna Turfan, in Chinese Turkestan. The work is a compilation of oral and written traditions recorded by Qurbānᶜalī from local inhabitants, and deals with both local history and especially lore connected with local Muslim saints and shrines. Other sections of the work deal with the history of the Dungans in the region as well.[92]

Qurbānᶜalī's other published work is a major monument of the Islamic historiography of imperial Russia, a 710-page compendium entitled the *Tawārīkh-i khamsa-yi sharqī*, which

---

89 Gosmanov, *Qauriy qaläm ezennän*, 317.
90 Gosmanov, *Qauriy qaläm ezennän*, 318.
91 Gosmanov, *Qauriy qaläm ezennän*, 318.
92 For a discussion of this work and its manuscript versions cf. H. F. Hofman, *Turkish Literature: a Bio-Bibliographical Survey* V (Utrecht, 1969), 75-78. Scholars who have cited this work include Ho-dong Kim, "The Cult of Saints in Eastern Turkestan—The Case of Alp Ata in Turfan," *Proceeding of the 35th Permanent International Altaistic Conference*, (Taipei, 1993), 199-226 and Masami Hamada, "Supplement: Islamic Saints and their Mausoleums," *Acta Asiatica* 34 (1978), 79-98.

was published in Kazan in 1910. The work contains numerous chapters, including treatments of the history of the khans of Qoqand, the history of Eastern Turkestan under the khojas, histories of Qulja and Chuguchak, a history of the Kazakh Middle Zhuz and the Nayman tribe, and a history of Semirech'e and the Ayaguz region under Russian rule. These sections are based primarily on oral sources. The work also contains sections dealing with ethnic history, treating the ethnic history of the Turkic peoples of imperial Russia, and of the Mongols. In addition, the work contains an extended ethnographic treatment of the Kazakhs of the Middle Zhuz. Other sections of the work include Qurbānᶜalī's account of the *ḥajj*, which he performed in 1897 and 1898, traveling from Chuguchak to Mecca via Omsk, Moscow, Warsaw, Vienna, Budapest, Sofia, Istanbul and Syria. There are also sections on the history of China and Japan, and a treatise on the Russo-Japanese War.[93]

In addition to his published works, Qurbānᶜalī also left several other major manuscript works. These include a 137-folio autograph located in the private collection of Mirkasyim Usmanov. This work contains a brief genealogical treatise about the Türkmān Bābā discussed above,[94] as well as the history of Semipalatinsk being featured in this publication. Additionally, the largest part of the autograph contains a draft biographical dictionary of the religious figures of eastern Kazakhstan, including Semipalatinsk, Karkaralinsk, the Semirech'e, and Chuguchak. The work is a major biographical dictionary and appears to be the only substantial biographical source for that region of the Islamic world.[95]

---

93 This major work has nevertheless been cited only rarely; cf. Karmysheva, "Kurbangali Khalidi," 102-109; B. Kh. Karmysheva and Dzh. Kh. Karmysheva, "Chto takoe Arka-iurt? (k istoricheskoi geografii Kazakhstana)," *Onomastika Vostoka*, (Moscow, 1980), 108-114; Togan, *Bügünkü Türkili (Türkistan) ve Yakın Tarihi*, 210, 250-253; 326-331.

94 Dzh. Karmysheva mentions a copy of what is evidently the same treatise as being located in the manuscript collection of the Academy of Sciences of the Kazakh SSR; cf. Karmysheva, "Kurbangali Khalidi," 101, n. 1.

95 For a brief discussion of this work cf. Gosmanov, *Qaurïy qaläm ezennän*, 322-325.

Qurbānᶜalī's history of Semipalatinsk has come down to us as an unfinished draft work and he appears to have been working on it as late as 1912, the year before his death. The draft contains two main sections, each dealing with the mosques and *imāms* of the city of Semipalatinsk, as well as with the general history of the city. There is a degree of repetition between the two sections; however, for the sake of avoiding a reorganization and rewriting of Qurbānᶜalī's draft, it was decided to leave the sections as they were, except for the completely identical sections, in order to minimize editing Qurbānᶜalī's work. The work as a whole is untitled, but the title Qurbānᶜalī chose for the second section was *Sīmī Pālāt baladasining bināsī wa Sīmī Pālāt nāmiyla wajh-i tasmīyasī wa ānda ōlān masjidlarning tārīkhī* (The building of the city of Semipalatinsk, the origin of the name Semipalatinsk and a history of the mosques that are in it). The work also contains a number of digressions that were not included in this publication for reasons of space. One such digression appears in the first section, and consists of a Muslim retelling of the Russian historical legend relating why the ruler of Kiev, Prince Vladimir, rejected Islam in favor of Christianity. The other digression appears at the end of the second section, and addresses themes of a political and religious nature not directly connected to Semipalatinsk. The editors hope that these important sections will be treated in separate publications.

As with his other works, Qurbānᶜalī only makes mention of oral sources, and his main source for this work appears to have been his teacher in Semipalatinsk, Mullā Mālik Afandī. In addition, he mentions several other figures from Semipalatinsk who lived in Chuguchak and who provided him with information. Nevertheless, Qurbānᶜalī's history is remarkable for its similarity, sometimes word for word, with Aḥmad-Walī's *Kitāb-i Tawārīkh-i Sīmīpūlāṭ Qalᶜa.* The relationship between the two works is quite unclear. Qurbānᶜalī cites Mullā Mālik in the chronological context of his own studies with this teacher, that is, in the 1860's and 70's, well before the compilation of the *Kitāb-i Tawārīkh-i Sīmīpūlāṭ Qalᶜa,* so it is not likely that the work was transmitted directly through that person, although the possibility that Mullā Mālik was a source for both histories cannot be ruled out. At the same time,

Qurbānᶜalī tells us in the *Tawārīkh-i khamsa-yi sharqī* that at one time he had been in direct correspondence with Aḥmad-Walī, and in that work he published the prologue of a letter addressed to him from this figure.[96] Whatever the relationship, Qurbānᶜalī's history was compiled twenty-four years after Aḥmad-Walī's and provides considerable supplemental information.

96 Qurbānᶜalī Khālidī, *Tawārīkh-i khamsa-yi sharqī*, 396–403.

[The First Mosque]

/1b/ The Russians first came to Semipalatinsk [and settled], and there was an island where the Qarasu River flows into the Irtysh. Seven households of Russians came there. They built houses out of wood, settled, and the Russians called this place "Sem' Palatka,"[97] or "Seven Wooden Houses." Later the word "palatka" changed to "palat." "Palatka" has the meaning of "wooden." Later when the Russians became numerous and there was no longer a danger of Kazakh raids, they left the island and built houses at the site of today's Vorstadt [suburb] and above it barracks were built. The Russians had first settled on the island in the 1750's and the building of houses of Sart merchants was in the 1790's.

Afterwards it was in the 1790's that Tatar merchants came and settled. When the Sarts and Tatars first came, they would generally perform the *namāz*es in the Toqal Mosque mentioned above.[98] After that the Tatars multiplied, and when there was one *maḥalla*, with leadership of Shafī Bāy Īshim ōghlī [ᶜAbdarrazzāqof], who was from the village of Mazarbashi[99] in the Kazan region, they built the First Mosque out of wood on the site of the present-day Stone Mosque. They made Aḥmad-Īshān Muḥammad ōghlī *imām*. He had studied in Bukhara and was licensed by Khalīfa Ḥusayn, may the mercy of God be upon him.[100] Later they had Muḥammadyār Ḥaḍrat Īshmuḥammad ōghlī of Mazarbashi come to assist this person and for [preparing] *fatwās* on *sharīᶜa* law; they made them joint *imāms* of this mosque.

The community continued to grow, and when there were two *maḥallas*, they moved the First Mosque to another place. /2a/ The name of the mosque that was moved is still the First Mosque. However, the mosque that was built on its [former]

---

97 The correct Russian form would be "*sem' palatok.*"

98 Rather, mentioned below.

99 See note 31.

100 See note 32.

location was registered as the Second Mosque. As for the number, after some discussion took place, the authorities, preferred Shafi's view and the mosque that was moved was registered as Number One and the one that was built in its place, Number Two. According to Mullā Mālik's account, this Second Mosque burned down in 1842, and the present-day Stone Mosque was built on its location. Although Mūsā Bāy of Qishqār[101] reportedly gave ten thousand silver rubles, when that ran out and more money was collected from the rich men of Semipalatinsk, it was completed. [This was] in the 1860's.

Muḥammadyār Ḥaḍrat took Aḥmad-Īshān's place, and was made *imām* to the mosque. He received his license during the time of Muḥammadjān Mufti.[102] This mosque was called the Muḥammadyār Ḥaḍrat Mosque, and later it was called the Faḍlallāh Mosque, after his son. In fact, when the mosque was first built, for a few years it would be named after the rich man who built it. But later it would jointly be called according to the name of its *imām* [as well], and finally, according to custom, the name of the rich man would no longer be used, and [only] that of the *imām* would be.

Muḥammadyār Ḥaḍrat came to Semipalatinsk in 1806, was co-*imām*, along with Aḥmad-Īshān for four years, and served as the [sole] *imām* in the First Mosque for twenty years. He died in the 1830's. After that, his son Mullā Faḍlallāh returned from Bukhara, took his father's place, and was *imām* for more than forty years. After that Muḥammad-ᶜAlīm b. Faḍlallāh returned from Qishqar. He served as *imām* for less than four years. After he was removed from office, Qārī ᶜUthmān b. Abū Bakr b. Shafī Bāy became the *imām*, in 1882. Qārī ᶜUthmān's name was Mahdī Yahūda. Because there was [already] someone with the same name, in Bukhara they would call him ᶜUthmān. He died in 1900, and at present Ibrāhīm b. Qārī ᶜAṭā became *imām* in his place.

The *mu'adhdhins* of the First Mosque were: first, Bashīr Mu'adhdhin, second Raḥmatallāh, third, Saydāsh, fourth,

---

101 See note 43.
102 See note 39.

Sayyid-ᶜAlī b. Saydāsh, fifth Ḥasan Mu'adhdhin b. Muḥammadyār Ḥaḍrat, sixth Aḥmad-Shāh b. Sayyid-ᶜAlī.

The Second Mosque

Aḥmad-Īshān was *imām* of this Second Mosque for fifty years and when he had grown old, he himself brought his son Ibrāhīm Makhdūm from Bukhara and made him *imām* in his father's place. He also earned the rank of *ākhūnd.* /2b/ After him they took his son-in-law Mullā ᶜUbaydullāh b. ᶜAbdalfayḍ, and following Ibrāhīm Ākhūnd's death in [blank] year they appointed him to the position of *imām.* In 1900 ᶜUbaydallāh died, and they placed his son ᶜAbdallāh Makhdūm in his place. Ḥājjī Fayda Aḥmad b. Ibrāhīm Ākhūnd became an assistant to ᶜAbdallāh. Such were the names of the five *imāms* of this Second Mosque.

In this mosque the first *mu'adhdhin* was Waddallāh, the second was Sayfaddīn, the third was Walī Mullā, the fourth was Ismāᶜil b. Aḥmad-Īshān, the fifth was Jalāladdīn b. Ismāᶜil, the sixth was Shāhī Mardān, the seventh was Aᶜẓām b. Shāhī Mardān.

/3a/

60 or 65 years after this [First] Mosque, that is, around 1270 AH [1853/54], (this was together with the Seventh Mosque, in the year 1852) the Tashkentian Mīr-Qurbān Bāy b. Ayyūb Bāy built a beautiful two-minaret mosque at his own expense, and they made someone named Ḥakīmjān Qārī the *imām.* When he approached the age of a hundred, he lost his reason, and one day while [performing the prayer as] *imām* at the *miḥrāb* he called out his wife by name. "Mūmāqān, did you tie up the calf?" Besides that, he was making all sorts of mistakes and omissions during the *namāz.* So they removed him and appointed in his place another Sart named Mullā Aḥmad-Jān Qārī b. Mullā Muslim b. Mu'minjān.

The original name of Mīr-Qurbān Bāy, who was the builder of the mosque, was truncated to Būqāch Bāy, and under this name he became well known. He possessed a hair of the Prophet Muḥammad, and he took good care of it up until his death, After his death, we heard that his sons gave it as a gift to Walī Bīy in Yarkend.[103] The story of this hair of the Prophet [is as follows]: He was given this relic by a Salar Dungan named Mullā Ismāᶜīl b. ᶜAbdarraḥmān. When this Dungan was on the *ḥajj*, and was in Istanbul he gave medical treatment to the mother of Sultan ᶜAbdalmajīd and when he cured her, the Sultan said, whatever you ask for, I will grant. Since he requested this relic, it was given to him. With this, he asked to be allowed to return to his home, and on his way to Semipalatinsk, he established a family in Kazan. When he decided to return to Kazan, he fell ill on the way in a Muslim village and died there. It was in 1274 AH [1857/58]. According to what Mullā Mālik Afandī said, he was a very pious and God-fearing *ṣāḥib-i nafas*.[104] May the mercy of God be upon him.

Because the Sarts were not subjects of Russia, when these two mosques that were described were first built, numbers were not assigned [to them] and in what order [they were built] is not known. They grew old and dilapidated. First, in the 1320's [1902-1911] Ḥājjī ᶜAlī Afandī Ḥusayn ōghlī renovated it.

/5b/ The account of the two mosques of the Sarts has already taken place. Now the order of the seven mosques which the important Kazanis built and their numbers will be related.

The Mosque that the Kazanis built after the Toqal Mosque, which we have already dealt with, was a wooden mosque on the site of today's Stone Mosque. Shafī Bāy spent a thousand paper rubles out of his own pocket, and according to Shafī Bāy's example money was collected. Because of Shafī Bāy's money this First Mosque was named after Shafī Bāy. As *imām* for this mosque they selected Aḥmad-Īshān b. Qizil-Muḥammad, who was originally from the village of Kötirnāj in the environs of Kazan and who had studied in Bukhara and

---

103 Presumably Dzharkent, the district center in Semirech'e *oblast'*, as opposed to Yarkend in Eastern Turkestan.

104 See note 78.

entered the Sufi path. Although this person had been licensed in the esoteric sciences by Khalīfa Ḥusayn, may the mercy of God be upon him, he had little training in the exoteric sciences. Because we had little connection in Russia's *sharīᶜa* affairs, a scholar who was strong in [*sharīᶜa*-related] issues and questions was needed. [Therefore] Shafī Bāy made them select a fellow villager from Mazarbashi, a kinsman and friend, Dāmullā Muḥammadyār Ḥaḍrat b. Īshmuḥammad, and he was *imām* jointly with Aḥmad-Īshān. According to Mullā Mālik's estimation, this mosque was built around 1800.

After that the Muslims multiplied, and when another *maḥalla* formed, they moved this First Mosque to the location of the Second Mosque, and on its site, under the leadership of Safqūl Bāy, they built a fine mosque out of wood, and made it bigger than the previous one. As before, the Shafī Bāy Mosque that was moved was registered as the First Mosque and this new mosque was called the Second Mosque. The *imām* of the First Mosque was this Muḥammadyār Ḥaḍrat. Qārī ᶜUthmān b. Abū Bakr ᶜAlī b. Shafī Bāy heard from his father and told us that the building and moving of this mosque took place around 1812. This Aḥmad-Īshān remained *imām* of the new Second Mosque. As for the First Mosque, it has been written that Aḥmad-Īshān and Muḥammadyār Ḥaḍrat were *imāms* jointly.

/6a/ Later, after the mosque had been moved, Muḥammadyār became the sole *imām*. Then his son Mullā Faḍlallāh returned from Bukhara during his father's lifetime and was *imām* with him jointly. Two years later, Muḥammadyār Ḥaḍrat died and Faḍlallāh became sole *imām*. Muḥammadyār Ḥaḍrat's death was some time in the 1830's. During Mullā Faḍlallāh's lifetime, his son Muḥammad-ᶜAlīm Makhdūm returned from Qishqar, where he had been studying with Dāmullā Ismāᶜīl Ḥaḍrat.[105] Even though he became *imām* in 1876 or 1877, he could not get along with the community and was removed from office. In 1882 Qārī ᶜUthmān b. Ḥājjī Abū Bakr b. Shafī Bāy b. Īshim was appointed *imām*. This person died around

[105] See note 42.

1900 and Ibrāhīm b. Qārī ^c Aṭā Kōkcheṭāwī was made *imām* in his place. During Qārī ^c Uthmān's time, the original mosque was renovated, beautified, and enlarged. When we returned from the *ḥajj*, that is, in 1898, it had reportedly been completed.

/6b/ According to what Mullā Mālik said, in 1841 the Second Mosque, which had been built on the site of the First Mosque, burned down. After that, with Aḥmad-Īshān's guidance, Mūsā Bāy of Qishqar gave thirty thousand paper rubles, and with that made plans for building a stone mosque. However, this money was insufficient for building the façade, and Mūsā Bāy did not give a second time. As for the wealthy men of Semipalatinsk, they were angry at the *īshān* and it was necessary to look for additional money. [They said:] "There is not enough money. What need was there to build a mosque out of stone?" Additional money was needed to make the outside out of stone. "Is it legally allowed for a second person to add to a first person's good deeds without permission?" they asked, and [they] would not give more, and they argued about it. As a result, the matter stalled for a while. At that time the police chief was a religious zealot named Vasil'evich. With zeal and resolution he took money from the rich men, whether they liked it or not, and finally completed the mosque. Out of fear of that police chief, the wealthy at first gave money very unwillingly, but after a while did give it willingly. It was a large and beautiful mosque, similar in appearance to the mosques of Istanbul. (They say there is no mosque in Russia like this one [except for] the mosque of Ḥājjī Ni^c matallāh Afandī in Tiumen'.)

Now, the first *imām* in this mosque was Aḥmad-Īshān; the second was his son Ibrāhīm Ākhūnd; the third was [Ibrāhīm Ākhūnd's] son-in-law ^c Ubaydallāh Hājjī b. Mullā Fayḍallah; the fourth was [^c Ubaydallāh's son] Mullā ^c Abdallāh Khulūṣī. His assistant and partner was Mullā Fayda-Aḥmad Hājjī b. Ibrāhīm Ākhūnd.

/8b/

The founding of the city of Semipalatinsk, the reason for its name, and a history of the mosques located there.

In the Name of God, the Compassionate, the Merciful

God is most knowledgeable.

In 1283 or 1284 AH, which corresponds to 1869, they said Prince Vladimir was coming and they prepared the city; we went out to see the festivities with Mullā Mālik Afandī and some of out colleagues, to the gate of the old fort, located between the old customs house and the Vorstadt. It was perfectly adorned. Flowers had been planted and banners had been sewn. At that time, Mullā Mālik related that this gate dated from Kalmyk times. It is the gate of a fort, and when the Russian first came, they stationed a few soldiers within this gate. (Later, before a church was built, they hung a bell on it.) Now the fort is in such a state, that within a few years it will be obliterated. But because its gate was made of baked brick, it has stood down to the present. But since it was close to collapsing, they put it up and showed it because of the prince's visit. They say that Küchüm Khan and his ancestors fought the Kalmyks here. He [Mullā Mālik] said whether Kalmyks or Küchüm and his ancestors had it built is unknown. But according to everyone, when the Russians came, this fort already existed. When we saw it its shape was still recognizable. Since Mullā Mālik was an informed person, he would tell long stories about this. He regretted the fall of Islam.

Then we placed ourselves on the high bank around the customs house. /9a/ When it came [time] to speak, I asked, "What is the origin of the name for this city, 'Semipalatinsk'?" In reply, he said that there was a well known island at the confluence of the Irtysh and Qarasu Rivers. Initially seven households of Russian fishermen came and built wooden shacks on this island. In summer they would come and fish, and in winter they would go away. The Russian called these seven houses

"Semi Palatka." Later, when soldiers came and stayed here, since there was no other current name for this place, it was still known as "Semi Palatka". However, they dropped the "ka" and so it became known as "Semi Palat". [In Russian] "Palatka" reportedly means a wooden house. [But] it is not unwarranted when others say that the name comes from seven large stone structures [*tashbulat*] that had been built there. They say that when the Russians arrived, the large stone buildings were still standing, and the wooden houses were not built for some time. This corresponds to the truth. If somebody claims that the name comes from "palat" then it is necessary to determine what the city was called before the building of the seven stone structures. It was after the city grew and the population became large that the large stone structures were established.

According to Mullā Mālik Afandī's estimation, it was in 1750 that the Russians first arrived here. When the Russians came, the original merchants from Ferghana and Turkistan were among the Kazakhs and they would bring in and trade livestock and goods with the Russian soldiers. After this became known to be profitable, one by one Tatar merchants began coming from the Kazan region and settled. /9b/ Within five or ten years there was a *maḥalla* and a Muslim congregation; they set out to build a mosque and spent money for this. They built a mosque without a minaret today called the Toqal Mosque. The Sarts, Kazakhs, and our own Tatars as well would perform the daily prayers and Friday prayers [there]. According to what Muḥammad-Razzāq Āka Pīr-Naẓarbāy ōghlī said, the year of this mosque's construction was 1794, while according to Qāsim Ākā Badal ōghlī it was in 1210 AH (1795-96). In the two accounts one said it according to the *hijra* date, and the other according to the Christian date, but the difference is only of a year or two. Both of them said that they had heard this from people who had been involved in the mosque's construction. This mosque's first *imām* was Sayyid-Burhān Īshān. After him it was someone called ^cAbbās Khān, and they indicated others who had been *imāms* without official appointments. They said that after them, someone named

Yāda or Jāda was *imām* for more than forty years. When this person died his age surpassed ninety. They say he was a pious and blessed person.

/10a/ Both of these narrators were born in the city of Semipalatinsk. Muḥammad-Razzāq Āka died in 1305 [1887/88] and Qāsim Āgha died in 1320 [1903/03] at the age of over 80, and they are buried in Chuguchak. Their fathers came to Semipalatinsk around 1200 AH [1785/86]. They said that Badal Ayyūb Bāy from among the Sarts, Īshimkān Bāy from among the Kazakhs, and Āqmurāt Bay from among the Tatars, were active in the mosque's construction.

/10b/

The Sarts' Second Mosque

The date of this mosque's construction has not been precisely determined, and the narrators differ between themselves by ten years. That is, some say it was in 1260 AH [1844/45], and others in 1270 AH [1853/54]. That is, it would be correct to say in the 1850's.

When the Tashkentian Mūqāch Bāy was *āqsaqāl*, he had the mosque built at his expense with two minarets. The first *imām* in this mosque was someone named Ḥakīmjān Qārī. When he approached the age of a hundred, they say he began to lose his reason. One day, when he was serving in the *miḥrāb*, he called his wife by name, and said "Mūmāqān, did you tie the calf?" And besides this, when he began being negligent and allowing mistakes in the *namāz*, they removed him and in his place they appointed the Sart Mullā Aḥmadjān Qārī b. Mu'minjān Bāy.

These two mosques are not under the supervision of the [Orenburg] Spiritual Assembly. Still those [Sarts] remained among the Kazakhs [were registered as Kazakhs], and do not submit *metricheskie knigi*, but only a *pamiatnaia kniga* is given by the district.[106] Births, deaths, marriages and divorces are recorded in them. But they say that in later years they became

[106] See note 70.

mixed among those who were registered among peasants and *meshchane*.[107]

This Mūqāch Bāy b. Ayyūb Bāy was first among the Sarts' wealthy men and was also their [blank] *āqsaqāl*.[108] His original name was Mīr-Qurmān. People say with regret that initially he was very wealthy, but later because of his son his wealth was lost.[109]

/11a/ The *mu'adhdhins* who were in this Second Mosque were: first Waddallāh, second Sayfaddīn, third Mullā Walīyallāh, fourth Ismāᶜīl, fifth Jalāladdīn b. Ismāᶜīl Mu'adhdhin, sixth Shāh-i Mardān.

The Third Mosque

After that, people from Kazan and [regions] south of it gathered, and when there was another *maḥalla*, in 1837 the rich men Ṭāhir and Ibrāhīm, the sons of ᶜAbdallaṭīf, who came from the village of Ulugh Mangar[110] and who were merchants in the Kazakh trade, built a beautiful wooden mosque at their own expense. As *imām* for this mosque, they chose Dāmullā ᶜĪsā Ibrāhīm ōghlī, who had studied the books and entered the Sufi path in Bukhara, and who was [also] from the village of Ulugh Mangar. They also built a *madrasa*, and this person became *mudarris* there. After his death in 1862, they made the *ḥāfiẓ* Aḥmad-Ṣafā Mullā al-Muḥammad ōghlī their *imām*. He was from one of the Chistopol' villages, and had been trained in Bukhara. When the first *madrasa* grew old and dilapidated this person had that *madrasa* torn down, and having raised money from the community, he built a stone *madrasa*. After Qārī Ṣafā's death in 1880, his younger brother Mullā Muḥsin Āghā became the designated successor. In 1882, after Mullā Muḥsin, Mullā ᶜAbdalḥaqq b. ᶜImādaddīn was appointed to the position of *imām*. In 1902 this mosque burned down and

---

107 See note 57.
108 See note 74.
109 The reading of this sentence is uncertain.
110 See note 45.

in its place Ṣādiqbāy Mūsīn built a beautiful Friday mosque. The building was erected by Ṣādiqbāy, but we heard that Ḥājjī ᶜAbdalqādir b. Khalīl Bāy Sayfullīn purchased and donated the land to enlarge the complex.

/11b/

Those who were *imāms* in this mosque: first ᶜĪsā Ḥaḍrat second Qārī Ṣafā, third Mullā Muḥsin, fourth ᶜAbdalbarr Ḥājjī. Those who were *mu'adhdhins* in this mosque: first, Iḥsān Mu'adhdhin, second Muḥammad-Ṣādiq b. Iḥsān, third Ṣāliḥ Mu'adhdhin, fourth ᶜAbdaljabbār b. Ṣāliḥ

The Fourth Mosque

Later the community still grew, and when the mosque came to be far away, the community pooled its money and in 1847 they built a mosque. They made Dāmullā Riḍā'addīn b. Mullā Walīd, who had studied the books to completion and had enetered the Sufi path in Bukhara, *imām* to this mosque. After this person's death, in 1880 they placed Mullā Aḥmadjān Sāᶜatchī ᶜUbaydallāh ōghlī,[111] who had been *mu'adhdhin* and the assistant, in the position of *imām*. He was one of the students of Yaᶜqūb Ḥaḍrat in Qishqar.[112] After [Mullā Aḥmadjān's] death, Mullā Faḍl Aᶜẓām b. Mullā Aḥmad-Walī was appointed in his place. During his tenure, in 1911, in the spring of 1329 AH, they purchased land next to the original mosque and added it onto [the mosque's lot], and they renovated and rebuilt [the mosque]. The first *mu'adhdhin* in this mosque was Nuᶜmān, the second was ᶜAbdalghafūr, the third was Mullā Aḥmadjān, who was mentioned, the fourth was Muḥammad-ᶜAlīm.

---

[111] The nickname "Sāᶜatchī" signifies either "watchmaker" or perhaps a person who determined the correct times for the prayers.

[112] See note 50.

/12a/

The Fifth Mosque

On the other side of the Irtysh River there is a settlement called Yataqlar.[113] There a wealthy Kazakh named Jūlāmān built a wooden mosque lacking a minaret. Although the construction of this mosque took place in 1827, that is, before the [construction of the] Third and Fourth Mosques that he have already dealt with, because it was done outside of official channels, it was given its number later, and its number was registered in the order it was received. Mullā ᶜAbdalkarīm b. Abū Bakr Kūgārchīnī was the unlicensed *imām*. Because the congregation's morals did not suit him and his character did not suit the people, after a year they removed him from the post of *imām*. In his place Mullā Muḥammad-Amīn Manṣūrof became *imām*. He was from among the Nizhnii Novgorod people, had studied in the *madrasa* in Machkara and had learned Qur'ān recitation from Ādā'ī Ḥaḍrat.[114] He received his license after a few years, and as a result the mosque received its number.

When this mosque grew old and dilapidated, money was collected by the *imām's* efforts from the community and in 1876 a large mosque was built out of wood. Muḥammad-Amīn was nicknamed Ṣārī Mullā. He fulfilled the duties of *imām* for more than fifty years. When he died after the construction of the new mosque, Mullā Ḥusāmaddīn b. Mullā Zaynalᶜābidīn, who had been the joint *imām*, became the sole *imām*. After a few years, he was removed from office, and one of his *shāgirds*, named [blank] was appointed.

Near to this mosque, the Kazakh Tlāw Bāy Ābdān ōghlī built a *madrasa*. They say the number of households making up the people of this mosque is 800. /12b/ 50 to 60 of these households are merchants, and the rest are all Kazakhs.

---

113 This name corresponds to a Kazakh social class. *Yataqs* were propertyless Kazakhs who lacked the means to nomadize; as a result, they were required to work as landless peasants and laborers.

114 See note 56.

As far as we know, this mosque's *mu'adhdhin* was Walīd, the father of Mullā ᶜAlī, *imām* of Ust'-Kamenogorsk. He was *mu'adhdhin* for a long time, and died at age 110, they say. The second *mu'adhdhin* was named Mullā ᶜAbdallāh.

The Sixth Mosque

In 1829 in the *maḥalla* adjacent to the Jūlāmān Mosque, Wāq Tinūbāy Kōgān ōghlī built a mosque and the first *imām* was a Kazakh named Bābājān. After that, someone named Niᶜmatjān, from Ufa district, became *imām*. In his time the mosque was given the number six. Then Mullā Aḥmadjān Āltay Bāy became *imām*. This *maḥalla* has 150 households, all of them Kazakhs.

The Seventh Mosque

The people multiplied, and in keeping with the custom for adding a new *maḥalla*, the people collected money, and in 1852 they built another mosque. The first *imām* was Mullā Zaynalᶜābidīn b. ᶜAbdalmannān from the village of Machkara, who had studied in Bukhara. After a few years, this person fell ill with paralysis, and the *mu'adhdhin* Muṣṭafā Saᶜīd ōghlī fulfilled the duties of *imām* for five years. After the *imām's* death in 1863, Mullā Faḍlallāh b. Niᶜmatallāh, who was from the village of Chalpu[115] in Ufa district and had studied in Bukhara, became *imām*. This person fell ill with tuberculosis, and in that year he died. In his place Dāmullā Aḥmad-Walī b. ᶜAlī Ūṭārī returned from Bukhara and became *imām* as well as *ākhūnd*. He left for the *ḥajj* in 1312 of the *hijra*, or in 1901, and died on the way in the city of Odessa. /13a/ His son Mullā Faḍlallāh-Akrām became his designated successor. In this mosque the first *mu'adhdhin* was Thābit Mullā, the second was Muṣṭafā Mu'adhdhin, the third was Muḥammadjān Mu'adhdhin b. Muṣṭafā.

---

[115] See note 60.

The Eighth Mosque

When the community had multiplied, yet another mosque was needed. In 1859, a rich man named ^c Atiyatallāh built a mosque and someone named Mullā Ḥusāmaddīn, who was from this village of Qāz[116] in the environs of Kazan, became *imām* to this mosque. Later Mullā ^c Abdaljabbār b. ^c Ubaydallāh, who trained in Bukhara and studied the books to completion and who was from the village of Muslim[117] became Mullā Ḥusāmaddīn's son-in-law and was designated to succeed him as assistant *imām*. After Ḥusāmaddīn's death, he became the sole *imām*. In 1881, or 1299 *hijra*, he went on the *ḥajj* and he died in Turkey on the way back, God's mercy be upon him. Until his son Ṣalāḥaddīn returned from Bukhara, before his return, Dāmullā Kamāladdīn, Mullā Mālik, and Mullā ^c Abdalḥaqq were the *imāms* for short intervals, and when Ṣalāḥaddīn [b. ^c Abdaljabbār] returned, he became *imām* in his father's place. This mosque's first *mu'adhdhin* was Ṣafī'allāh, and the second was ^c Ubaydallāh, the third was [blank].

/13b/

The Ninth Mosque

The community still grew, and after the mosque became too distant, in 1882, which was 1300 *hijra*, Ḥājjī Muḥammadjān Bāy Ishtirākof, who was from the village of Tashkichü,[118] built a beautiful mosque. Dāmullā Kamāladdīn b. Muḥammad-Raḥīm was appointed *imām* and *mudarris* to it. This person studied initially in Qishqar with Dāmullā Ismā^c īl Ḥaḍrat, and then trained in all of the sciences in Bukhara. In this mosque the *mu'adhdhin* is ^c Ubaydallāh. He had been designated to succeed Ṣafī Mu'adhdhin of the Eighth Mosque.

---

116 See note 65.

117 This village probably corresponds to Muslim, officially known as Musliumkino, today located in Chistopol' raion, Tatarstan.

118 See note 69.

As of this year of 1330, or 1912 there are nine mosques under the supervision of the [Orenburg] mufti and two [other] mosques are called Chala Kazakh or Sart mosques. They are described in the passage on the Sarts. One of them is without a minaret and the other has twin minarets. According to the accounts of trustworthy informants, this year there are thirty thousand [inhabitants] and the number of structures approaches four thousand. There are two sections [of the city]. It is one of the most prosperous Muslim cities in Russia after Kazan and Orenburg. Up until approximately the year 1300 [1882/83] its people did not divorce themselves from the old manners of comportment and although they were restrained and were not extravagant, they say that since this date there have been many changes.

The Toqal Mosque had not been restored or renovated since it was built. This was because the *maḥalla* had no one who was wealthy, and a permit to restore and renovate the mosque was not obtained from the government, since /14a/ the idea had been to hinder it because probably it had been originally built without permission. But, it will be recalled, up until 1328 AH it was opposed and [the mosque] became dilapidated. In that year, which is 1910, we heard that it was beautifully restored and renovated by the authoritative notable Ḥājjī ᶜAlī Afandī Ḥājjī Aḥmadī ōghlī Ḥusaynof. May the Lord accept his good deed!

For each of the numbered mosques that have been described, there are *maktabs* and *madrasas*. But the Toqal Mosque and the Būqāch Bāy Mosque have no *madrasas*. Until 1325 AH [1907/08] the *uṣūl-i qadīm* was studied in the *madrasas* and in that year some children's schools and also a few *maktabs* were established. Although the *uṣūl-i jadīd* was started, it was in 1330 AH [1912] that the term *uṣūl-i jadīd* was dropped in the *madrasa* of the Stone Mosque and people thought it more suitable to have [the children] taught according to the old method.

\1b\ سیمی پالاد بلده سینه اوّل روسلر کلوب اینک اوّل ایرتش صوی قرا
صو ایله اورتالغنده بر جزیره آرال باردور آنکا یتی اویلوک روس کلوب
تاقته دن اوی یصوب اوترمشلرده بونکا روسلر سیم پالاتقه یعنی تاقته دن
صالنمش یتی اوی اسمنی دیروب صونکره پالاتکه اسمی پالات دیه
آلنمش پالاتکه تاقته معناسنده دور \\ صونکره ینه روسلر کوبایوب
قضاق چپاولندن ایمیس اولوردای بولغاچ جزیره دن چتب اوشبو کونکی
فرشتات اورننه اویلر صالیب یوقاروسنه عسکرخانه کازارمه صالنمش لردر
روسلرننک ابتدا آرالغه کلوب اوتورولری ۱۷۵۰نچی سنه لر ایچنده
اولب سوداکر سرة لرننک اوی صالیب اوتورولری

۱۷۹۰نچی یل لرده دور بعده نوغای سوداکر دخی کلوب اورناشوب
اوّلده سرة نوغای کلسی یوقاروده یازلمش توقال مسجدده نماز اوقوب
تورمشلر \\ بعده نوغای لر کوبایوب برر محله لیک بولدقده قزان قربـ
سی مزارباشی آوللنک شفی بای (ایشم اوغلی) اجتهادی ایله اوشبو
کونکی تاش مسجد اورننه یغاچ دن ۱نچی نومر مسجد صالنغانلر \\
بونکا بخارادا تحصیل قیلغان هم خلفه حسین علیه الرحمةدن مرخص
بولغان احمد ایشان محمد اوغلی عبد الرزقف نی امام قیلغانلر \\ بعده
بو ذاتقه معین لیک اوچون و هم احکام شرعیه ده فتوی اوچون ینه
مزارباشی ننک محمدیار حضرت ایشمحمد اوغلنی آلدریب مذکور
مسجدکه مشترک امام قیلغانلر \\ جماعت ینه کوبایوب ایکی محله لیک
بولدقدن بو برنچی نومر مسجدینی ایکنچی طرفغه کوچرمش لر ده...
\2a\ کوچرلمش مسجد هنوز ۱نچی نومرده بولب اننک اورننه صالنمش
مسجد ۲نچی نومرده یازلمش \\ لکن نومرخصوصنده برآز کفت گو
بولمش ایسه ده شفی بای ننک سوزنی حکومت ترجیح قیله رق
کوچرلمش مسجد ۱نچی نومرده اورننه صالنمش مسجد ۲نچی نومرده

اولمشدر \\ بو ۲نچی نومر مسجد ملّا مالک ننک نقلنه نظراً
۱۸۴۲نچی میلادیه ده یانوب اورننه اوشبو کونکی تاش مسجد بنا
قیلندی\\ تاش مسجدکه قشقارننک موسی بای اون منک صوم کموش
ویرمش ایسه ده او آقچه کفایه ایتمدکدن صونکره سیمی بایلرندن آقچه
جمع اوله رق تمام اولدی ۱۸۶۰نچی سنه لر ایچنده احمد ایشان اوز
اورننده محمدیار حضرت کوچرلمش مسجدکه امام تعیین قیلنوب
محمدجان مفتی ایامنده اوکاز آلغان \\ بو مسجد محمدیار حضرت
مسجدی صونکره اوغلی فضوله حضرت مسجدی دیه شهرتلنمش زیرا
ابتدا مسجد بنا قیلندقده بای ننک اسمی ایله برآز یل لر سویلنوب بعده
امامی ایله مشترک ذکر قیلنه رق صونکره بای اسمی متروک امام اسمی
مشهور اولمق عادتدندر\\

محمدیار حضرت ۱۸۰۶نچی یلده سیمی که کلوب ۴ یل احمد ایشان
ایله شریک امام بولب ۱نچی نومر مسجده ۲۰ یل مقداری امام بولب
بعده ۱۸۳۰نچی یل لر ایچنده وفات بولدی \\ بعده اوغلی ملّا فضوله
بخارادن قایتوب آتاسی اورننه قرق یلدن آرتوغراق امام بولب توردی
بعده محمد علیم بن فضوله قشقاردن قایتوب دورت یلغه یتار یتماس
امامتلیک قیلب معزول اولدقدنصنکره ۱۸۸۲نچی یلده قاری عثمان بن
ابو بکر بن شفی بای محراب نشین بولدی\\ قاری عثماننک اسمی
مهدی یهودا ایدی یهودا اسمنه مشابهتدن نقرة ایله بخاراده عثمان
اسمنی دیرمشلر \\ ۱۹۰۰نچی سنه لرده وفات ایدب حالا اورننه ابراهیم
بن قاری عطا امام بولدی ۱نچی مسجد مؤذنلری ۱نچی بشیر مؤذن
۲نچی رحمه الله ۳نچی سیداش ۴نچی سید علی ابن سیداش ۵نچی
حسن مؤذن ابن محمدیار حضرت ۶نچی احمد شاه ابن سید علی دور
یازلمش ۲نچی نومر مسجدده احمد ایشان ۵۰ یل لر مقداری امام بولب
توروب تمام قارتایغاچ بخارادن اوغلی ایبراهیم محذوم نی اوز اورننه
امام قویدی آخوندلیق رتبه سنی دخی جائز اولدی

\2b\ بعده بوننک دامادی ملّا عبیدالله ابن دملّا عبدالفیض معین‌لیک آلیب یل ابراهیم آخوندننک وفاتی ایله امامتلیککه نصب قیلدی \\ ۱۹۰۰نچی سنه‌لرده عبیدالله دخی وفات بولب اوغلی عبدالله محذوم خلوصی آتاسی جاینه اوتوردی حاجی فیده احمد ابن ایبراهیم آخوند عبدالله‌غه معین بولدی \\ بو ۲نچی نومر مسجدده نام‌لری مذکور بش عدد امام بولدی‌لر بو مسجدده ۱نچی مؤذن ودّالله ۲نچی سیف‌الدین ۳نچی ولی ملّا ۴نچی اسماعیل ابن احمد ایشان ۵نچی جلال‌الدین ابن اسماعیل ۶نچی شاهی‌مردان ۷نچی اعظم بن شاهی مردان مؤذن‌در

\3a\ (۷نچی نومر مسجد ایله برابر ۱۸۵۲نچی یلده اولور بو مسجددن ۶۰ یاخود ۶۵ یل‌لر صونکره یعنی ۱۲۷۰چی هجریه‌لر حدودنده) تاشکندی میر قربانبای ابن ایوب بای اوز کیسه‌سندن صرف ایدب ایکی مناره‌لی بر کوزل مسجد صالیب بونکا حکیم‌جان قاری نامنده بر ذاتی امام قویدیلر \\ یاشلری یوزکه یاقنلادقده عقلدن یازیب بر کون محرابده امام ایکن خاتونی‌ننک اسمیله چاقریب \\ موماقان بوزاونی بایلادنکمه \\ دیوب و بوندن غیری دخی نمازده سهو و خطالری کوبایدکدن بونکا تعطیل ویروب اورننه ینه سرد طائفه‌سندن ملّا احمدجان قاری ابن ملّا مسلم ابن ملّا مؤمن‌جان منصوب بولدی \\ بانی مسجد اولن مر قربان بای‌ننک اصل اسمی منحوت ایدیلوب بوقاچ بای دیه مشهور اولمش ایدی \\ بو ذاتده بر موی مبارک اولوب اوزی‌ننک وفاتنه قدر کوزل تربیه قیلنب توردی وفاتندن صونکره اوغل لری یرکندده ولی بایغه هدیه ایتدیکی مسموع مزدور\\

بو موی مبارک ملّا اسماعیل بن عبدالرحمن نامنده بر صالاری دونکانیدن هدیه قیلنمش ایدی\\ مذکور دونکانی حج سفرنده اسلامبوله کلوب سلطان عبدالمجیدنک آناسینه دوا قیلوب شفایوب

اولدقدن سلطان هر نه صوراسه برور ایکان بو ذات بر موی مبارک
التجا ایتدکندن برلمش دور \\ بوننکله مملکتنه قایتمق آرزو ایدب
سیمی پالاده کلدکده قزانده جماعتنی آلیب بیله کتمک مصلحت
کورلوب قزانغه قایتدغنده یولده بر مسلمان آولنده خسته لنوب آنده
وفات ایتمشدر ۱۲۷۴ نچی سنه لرده \\ ملّا مالک افندی ننک ایتوی
بوینچه کوب دیندار صاحب نفس متقی ذات ایدی دیوردی \\ خدا
رحمت ایلیه \\

بو یازلمش ایکی مسجد سردیه اهالیسی روسیه یه تابع اولمزدن اوّل
صالنوب نومر تحتنه داخل اولمامشلر ایدی حالانه تارتیبکا اولدیغی معلوم
دکلدر ایسکی لنوب فنایه قریب اولمش ایکان اوّلده توقال مسجدنی
۱۳۲۰ نچی سنه لرده حاجی علی افندی حسین اوغلی تجدید ایلمش در
\\

\5b\ سردیه اهالیسی ننک اسمنده ایکی مسجدننک بیانی یازیلوب و
یتی قزانلی آغای بای لرنک بنا قیلدیغی مساجدلر ترتیبی نومرلری ایله
تحریر ایلدیلر \\

یازلمش توقال مسجددن صونکره قزان لی لرنک صالغان مسجدلری ننک
اینک اوّلی اوشبو کونکی تاش مسجد اورننده بر آغاچ مسجد ایدی \\
بو مسجدنی شفی بای اوز کسه سندن منک صوم سکناسنی چقاریب ینه
شفی بای ننک دلالتی ایله آقچه جیولوب شفی بای و هم باشچی سی
دخی بولدیغچون بو مسجد شفی بای اسمنده ۱ نچی نومر مسجد
آتالمشدر بونکا بخاراده تحصیل قیلغان و دخل سلوک بولغان اصلی
قزان نواحیسندن کترناج اسملی قریه ننک احمد ایشان قزل محمد
اوغلی نی امام قیلدیلر بو ذات علم باطنده خلفه حسین علیه الرحمة دن
مرخص ایسه ده علم ظاهرده خطی آز ایدی زور اولدقدن او وقتده روسیه

ننک شرع شریف ایشلرینه قاتشوی آز اولدیغچون مسئله مسائل که ماهر
بر عالم لازم اولوب مذکور شفی بای اوزی ننک آولداشی هم خویش و
قرداشی مزارباشی ننک دملّا محمدیار حضرت ایشمحمد اوغلنی آلدریب
احمد ایشان ایله مشترک امام قیلمشلر بو مسجدننک بناسی ملّا مالک
ننک تخمینی بوینچه ۱۸۰۰نچی یل لر حدودنده دور \\ بعده مسلمانلر
کوبایوب ینه بر محله لیک بولغاچ اوشبو ۱نچی نومر مسجدنی ۲نچی
جایغه کوچریب آننک اورننه سفقول بای باشچی اولاراق یغاچدن یخشی
ایتب اوّلکی دن الوغراق بر مسجد صالغانلر \\ کوچرلکان شفی بای
مسجدی بورونغی چه ۱نچی نومر بو ینکی مسجد ۲نچی نومر دیه
یازلمش ۱نچی نومر مسجدکه مذکور محمدیار حضرت امام بولمشدر بو
مسجدننک کوچریلوب صالنوی ۱۸۱۲نچی یل لر حدودنده اولدیغنی
قاری عثمان بن ابو بکر علی ابن شفی بای آتاسندن اشتمش بزه
سویلمش \\ ۲نچی نومر ینکی مسجدکه بیاغی احمد ایشان امام بولب
قالمش ۱نچی نومر مسجدکه اوّل امام احمد ایشان و محمدیار حضرت
اشتراکله توردیغی یازلوب کچدی

\6a\ بعده مسجد کوچرلکاچ محمدیار حضرت مستقل امام بولدی بعده
اوغلی ملّا فضولله حضرت آتاسی ننک حیاتنده بخارادن قایتوب مشترک
امام بولدیغندن ایکی یل صونکره محمدیار حضرت وفات اولب فضولله
حضرت مستقل امام بولدی \\ محمدیار حضرت ننک وفاتی ۱۸۳۰نچی
یل لر ایچنده دور \\ ملّا فضولله ننک دخی حیاتنده اوغلی محمد علیم
مخدوم قشقار قریه سنده داملّا اسماعیل حضرتدن اوقوب قایتوب
۱۸۷۶نچی یلده یاخود ۷نچی یلده امام بولمش ایسه ده قوملری ایله
چغوشالمیوب معزول اولدیده ۱۸۸۲نچی یلده قاری عثمان بن حاجی ابو
بکر بن شفی بای بن ایشم امام نصب قیلندی \\ بو ذات ۱۹۰۰نچی
یل لر حدودنده وفات اولب حالا اورننه ابراهیم بن قاری عطا کوکچه
طاوی امام دور \\

قاری عثمان ایامنده اوّلکی مسجد تجدید و تزیین و توسعه ایدلدی بزم
حج دن قایتقوشمزدن یعنی ۱۸۹۸نچی یلده تمام بولمش ایدی \\

بو برنچی نومر مسجدده اوّل مؤذن بشیرآغا دیدیکی بر ذات ۲نچی
رحمة الله ۳نچی سید علی ۴نچی سیداش ۳نچی حسن مؤذن ابن
محمدیار حضرت ۶نچی احندشاه ابن سید علی حسن مؤذن برلن
مشترک توردیلر

\6b\ مذکور ۱نچی نومر مسجد اورننه صالنغان ۲نچی نومر مسجد ملّا
مالک ننک ایتونچه ۱۸۴۱نچی یلده اوت قضاسی ایله تمام یانوب بتدی
\\ بعده احمد ایشان ننک دلالتی ایله قشقارننک موسی بای اوتوز منک
سکناتسی آقچه بروب بوننکله مسجدنی تاشدن قیلمغه مباشرة ایتدی
لکن طرح فصادنه بو آقچه آزلیق قیلیب موسی بای ایکنچی دفعه آقچه
برمادی سیمی بای لری ایشانغه اوفکانی قیلب آقچه ننک یتوشنه قرامق
کرک ایدی آقچه یتماز ایکان مسجدنی تاشدن قیلمق نی حاجت ایدی
دیب تاشدن اولدقده فصادنی آقچه غه لایق یاصاتمق لازم ایدی بر
آدمنک خیراتنه اجازتسز ایکنچی آدمنک قوشولمغی شرعاً جائزمی دیه
آقچه برماس یا غنه مسئله مسائل لر سویلب حاصل برنچه وقت لر
توقتالب توردی \\ بو حین ده بزیلاویچ اسملی بر غیور ذات پالیتسه
میستر بولوب آننک غیرة و همتی ایله بای لردن استر استمز آقچه آلیب
مسجدنی اتمامه ایرشدی \\ مذکور پالیتسه مسترننک قورقتوب کوچلوی
بوینچه بایلر اوّلده آقجه بیک رانجوب برسه لرده تمامنده صونکره آفرین
که یولقدی \\ استنبول جامع لری طرزنده کوزل بر بیوک مسجد بولدی
حالا (بو جامع تومنده حاجی نعمة الله افندی جامعی بو ایکی معادل
روسیه ده جامع یوقدر دیرلر) بو مسجده اوّل امام احمد ایشان ۲نچی
آننک اوغلی ابراهیم آخوند ۳نچی بوننک دامادی عبیدالله حاجی ابن

ملّا فیض الله ۴نچی بوننک اوغلی ملّا عبدالله خلوصی معین و شریکی ملّا فیده احمد حاجی ابن ایبراهیم آخونددور \\

\8b\ سیمی پالات بلده سی ننک بناسی و سیمی پالات نامیله وجه تسمیه سی و آنده اولن مسجدلرنک تاریخی

بسم الله الرحمن الرحیم

الله اعلم تاریخ هجری ایله ۱۲۸۳نچی یا ۴نچی سنه ایدی که میلادیه ۱۸۶۹نچی یل پادشاه ننک اوغلی کناز ولادیمر کلور دیه شهری توزاتمشلر ایدی اوشبو آداقده ملّا مالک افندی و بر نچه شرکالرمز ایله بزانمش جایلری تماشایه چقب ایسگی تاموجنی ایله فرشتاد آراسنده اولن کمنه قورغاننک داربازاسنه واردق کمال زینت ایله زینت لب کل لر اوتورتمش بایراقلر تکمش \\ شول حینده ملّا مالک افندی سویلدیکه بو داربازه قلماق زماننده قالمش قورغاننک داربازه سیدرکه ابتدا روسیه کلدکده برآز عسکر اوشبو قورغاننک ایچنده تورمشلر (صونکره چرکاو صالننه قدر بونکا کلاکولده آصمشلر) شمدی قورغان بو حالا کلمش که برآز یلدن اثری دخی محو اولور داربازه سی پشق خشتدن اولدیغچون بو وقته قدر تورمشدر بوده یقلمیه یاقنلامش ایدی پادشاه اوغلی کلمک مناسبتیله توزاتمشلر \\ بوراده کوچوم خان و آننک بابالری قلماق ایله محاربه قیلمش ایمش قلماق صوقغانمی یاخود کوچوم خان و آننک بابالری صوقغانمی آنیسی معلوم دکلدر ایدی \\ هرچه بو قورغان روسیه کلدکده موجود اولب بزلر کوردکمزده حین دخی سرداری بلنور ایدی \\ ملّا مالک معلوماتلی ذات اولدقدن بو بابده اوزاق حکایه لر سویلدی \\ اسلامنک تنزلندن تاسفلر ایلدی \\ آندن تاموجنی قاشنده بیوک یار اوستنه اولتردوق سوز موردی کلدکده صوردمکه \\ \9a\ بو شهرنک

سیمی پالاد اسمنه وجه تسمیه نه دور \\ او کورلمش جزیره آرال که
ایرتش آغمی ایله قرا صوونک فاصله سیدور \\ اوّلده یتی اویلوک
بالقچی روسلر کلوب شول آرالده تاقته دن باله غان یصاب یاز کلوب
بالق آولاب قش قایتوب یورمشلر \\ شول تاقته دن یصالمش یتی اوینی
روسلر سیم پالاتکه دیه سویلیوب صونکره عسکر کلوب توشدکده دخی
بو اورن ننک باشقه بر معیّن اسمی اولمامغله همان بیاغی "سیم پالاتکه"
اسمی اشتهار فقط "ک" ساقط اوله رق "سیمی پالات" دیه افتخار
ایدلمش "پالاتکه" تاقته دن یاصالمش اویی دیمکدر \\ بعض لرنک زعم
ایتدیکی کبی دکلدرکه یتی تاشبولات صالنمشده آندن بو اسم آلنمش
\\ روس کلدیغی وقت تاشبولات شویله تورسون بر نچه یل لرغه چه تاقته
توبه لی اویده کورلمامشدر \\ و هم توغرسیده بودور \\ اکر "پالات"
اسمی ادّعا ایدن وار ایسه یدی تاشبولات بناسندن اقدم شهرنک نه
اسمی سویلندکنی اثبات لازم کلور تاشبولات شهر بیوکلنوب اهالی
کوبایدکدن صونکره اولن کارلردندر \\ ملّا مالک افندی ننک تخمینی
بوینچه روسلر نک بو جایه اوّل قدم قویدیغی ۱۷۵۰نچی یل لر ایچنده
دور \\ روسلر کلدیکی ایله قضاق ایچنده بورون فرغانه و ترکستان
سوداکرلری روسیه عسکریه مال و اشیا کرکوزوب صاتیب آشنالیق پیدا
ایتدکدن صونکره برلب ایکی لب کریب و هم قزان طرفلرندن نوغای
سوداکرلری دخی کلوب استقامت قیلب \9b\ بش اون یل ایچنده بر
محله مسلمان جمع اوله رق مسجد بناسنه تشبث ایدب آقچه چغارمشلر
اوشبو کونکی توقال مسجد اسمنده اولن مناره سز مسجدنی بنا قیلنمشلر
سردیه و قضاقیه و بزم اهالیء نوغای دخی اول مسجدده نماز جماعت و
جمعه اوقوب تورمشلر دیدی \\ محمد رزاق اکه پر نظربای اوغلی
نقلنچه ۱۷۹۴نچی میلادیه ده \\ قاسم آغه بدل اوغلی ننک دیدکنچه
۱۲۱۰نچی هجریه ده دور \\ بری میلادیه و بری هجریه ایله سویلدیکه
ایکسی ننک خبرنده فقط بر ایکی یل تفاوة اولور \\ هر ایکسی مسجد
بناسی ننک ایچنده اولن ذواتلردن ایشتدکی سویلدی \\ بو مسجدده اوّل

امام سید برهان ایشان و بعده عباس خان دیه بر ذاتلر و غیری لر بلا تعیین امام بولوب اوتکازمشلر \\ بونلردن صونکره "یدا" یاخود "جادا" نامنده بر ذات قرق یلدن زیاده امام اولدیغنی سویلیورلر \\ بو آدم نک یاشی توقساندن تجاوز ایدب وفات اولمش \\ متقی متبرک ذات ایدی دیورلر \\

\10a\ مذکور ایکی راوی هر برلری سیمی پالات بلده سنده توغوب محمد رزاق اکه ۱۳۰۵نچی هجریه قاسم آغه ۱۳۲۰نچی هجریه لرده یاشلری ۸۰دن آشوب چوچکده مدفون اولدیلر آتالری ۱۲۰۰ هجریه حدودنده سیمی که کلوب مسجدنک بناسنه سردلردن بدل بای ایوب بای اوغلی قضاقدن ایشمکان بای نوغایلردن آقمورت بایلر مباشر اولدقلرینی آتالرندن آغالرندن سویلدیلر \\

\10b\ سردلرننک ۲نچی مسجد

بو مسجدننک بناسی سنه سی جزماً تعیین ایدلمیوب روایت ایدوچی لر آراسنده اون یلده زیاده تفاوت سویلیورلر یعنی بعض لر منک ایکی یوز ۶۰نچی سنه لرده و بعض لرده ۷۰نچی سنه لر ایچنده صالنمش دیرلر \\ یعنی میلادیه ده ۱۸۵۰نچی سنه لر ایچنده توغری کلور \\ بو مسجدنی تاشکندلیک موقاچ بای اقسقال لیق وقتنده اوز خرجتی ایله ایکی مناره لی قیلوب صالدرمشدر \\ بو مسجدده ۱نچی امام حکیم جان قاری نامنده بر ذات اولوب یاشلری یوزکه قریب کلدکده عقلدن برآز یازه توشدیکنی سویلیورلر \\ بر کون محرابده امام بولوب توروب خاطونی ننک اسملی ایله چاقرب موماقان بوزاونی بایلادنکمه دیدیکی بوندن غیری دخی نمازده سهو خطالری اوله باشلادقده بونکا تعطیل ویروب اورننه ینه سرة طائفه سندن ملّا احمد جان قاری ابن مؤمن جان بای منصوب اولمشلر \\ بو ایکی مسجد اهالیسی صوبرانیه غه قرامیوب هنوز

قضاق قتارنده تورمشلر متریکه دفتر برلمیوب اویازدن پاموتنی کناگه
بریلوب توغان اولگان نکاح طلاق اهل لری شونکا یازیلوب تورلور \\
امّا صونکراق یل لرده بعضاً کرستیان مشچان قتارنده یازلغانلریده
بولغانلادی دیه سویلدیلر \\ مذکور موقاچ بای ابن ایوب بای سیمی
سرة لری ننک ۱نچی بایی و هم ... نچی اقسقالی ایدی اصل اسمی میر
قورماندر \\ اوّلده خیلی دولتمند اولوب صونکره زوالنه دولتنه سبب
اوغلی اشکه اولدیغنی تاءسافله سویلیورلر

\11a\ بو ۲نچی نومر مسجدده مؤذن اولنلر ۱نچی وَدّالله ۲نچی سیف
الدین ۳نچی ملّا ولی الله ۴نچی اسماعیل ابن احمد ایشان ۵نچی جلال
الدین ابن ایسماعیل مؤذن ۶نچی شاه مردان ۷نچی اعظم بن شاه مرداندر

۳نچی مسجد

بعده اتراف قزاندن و بو جانبده یورن لردن جیولوب ینه بر محله خلق
بولدقده الوغ منکار قریه سی ننک قزاقچی سوداکرلرندن طاهر و ابراهم
بایلر عبد اللطیف اوغل لری اوز کیسه لرندن چقاریب ۱۸۳۷نچی یل
لرده یغاچدن بر کوزل مسجد بنا قیلدیلر \\ بونکا بخاراء شریفده
تحصیل قیلغان ختم کرده و هم داخل سلوک بولغان ینه منکار قریه سی
ننک دملّا عیسی ابراهیم اوغلنی امام قیلدیلر بر مدرسه دخی بنا ایدب
مذکور ذات آنکا مدرس بولدی \\ بو ذاتنک وفاتی بعدندن
۱۸۶۲نچی یل لرده بخاراده تحصیل قیلغان حافظ کلام الله چستای قریه
لرندن احمد صفا ملّا المحمد اوغلی امامتلک که اوتوردی \\ اوّلکی
مدرسه ایسکروب فنا حالنه کلدکده بو ذات اول مدرسه نی یقیب اورننه
جماعت دن آقچه چقاریب بر طاش مدرسه بنا ایلدی \\ ۱۸۸۰نچی یل
لر ایچنده قاری صفا ننک وفاتی ایله آننک بر توغمه اینوسی ملّا محسن
آغاسی ننک جای نشینی بولدی ۱۸۸۲نچی یلده ملّا محسندن صونکره

ملّا عبدالحق ابن عمادالدين امامتلک که نصب قیلندی \\ ۱۹۰۲نچی یلده بو مسجد یانوب اورننه صادقبای موسین بر کوزل جامع بنا ایتمش \\ مسجدنک بناسی صادقبایدن امّا اورننی اطرافدن توسعه قیلب حاجی عبدالقادر ابن خلیل بای سیف اللین آلیب بردیغی مسموعمز اولدی \\ بو مسجدده امام اولنلر اوّل عیسی حضرت ۲نچی قاری صفا ۳نچی ملّا محسن ۴نچی عبدالبرّ حاجی دور \11b\ بو مسجدده مؤذن اولنلر اوّل احسان مؤذن ۲نچی محمد صادق ابن احسان ۳نچی صالح مؤذن ۴نچی عبدالجبار ابن صالح

۴نچی نومر مسجد

بعده ینه جماعت کوبایوب مسجد یراقلق قیلغاچ جماعت اوزلری آقچه جیوشوب ۱۸۴۷نچی یل لرده بر مسجد بنا قیلدیلر بو مسجد که بخاراء شریفده تحصیل و هم سلوک قیلغان ختم کرده دملّا رضاءالدین بن ملّا ولید امام بولدی \\ بو ذات آننک وفاتی بعدنده ۱۸۸۰نچی یل ده مؤذن و معین بولب تورغان قشقارده یعقوب حضرتنک تلمیذلرندن ملّا احمدجان ساعتچی عبیدالله اوغلی امامتلیک که اوتوردی \\ بوننک وفاتی بعدنده ملّا فضل اعظم ابن ملّا احمد ولی بو اورنغه منصوب بولدی \\ بوننک ایامنده ۱۹۱۱نچی یل هجریه ۱۳۲۹نچی یازنده اوّلکی مسجدنک اطرافندن یر آلیب قوشولوب ینکی دن تعمیر و تجدید ایدلمشدر \\ بو مسجده اوّل مؤذن نعمان ۲نچی عبدالغفور ۳بچی ملّا احمدجان مذکور ۴نچی محمد علیم

\12a\ ۵نچی نومر مسجد

ایرتیش صوی ننک ایکنچی یاغنده یاتاقلر اسملی بر قریه اولوب بونکا قضاق طائفه سندن جولامان اسملی بر بای مناره سز بر یغاچ مسجد بنا

قیلب بو مسجدنک بناسی ۱۸۲۷نچی یل لرده یعنی یوقارغی یازلمش ۳نچی نومر ۴نچی نومر مسجدلردن مقدم ایسه ده حکومتدن امر و فصاد ایله اولمدقدن نومری صونکره یه قالوب نومره داخل اولدیغی وقتنده ترتیب ایله یازلدی \\ بونکا بخاراء شریفده تحصیل قیلب قایتقان ملّا ابدالکریم بن ابوبکر کورکاچینی اوکازسز امام بولمش ایسه ده اهالی ننک اخلاقی آنکا آننک خلقی اهالینه اویوشمیوب برار یلدن صونکره اوزینی امامتلکدن خارج قیلدی \\ اورننه نیژغورتسکی طائفه سندن مچکاره مدرسه سنده تحصیل قیلغان آداءی حضرتدن قراءة ایتکان ملّا محمد امین منصورف امام بولدی \\ بر نچه یلدن صونکره اوکاز آلیب بوننکله مسجد نومر عددنه داخل بولدی \\ مذکور مسجد ایسکوروب توزوب فنا حالنه یاقنلاشدقدن امامنک اجتهادیله جماعتدن آقچه جیولوب ۱۸۷۶نچی یل بر بیوک مسجد یغاچدن بنا ایدلدی \\ محمد امین صاری ملّا ایله ملقب ایدی ۵۰ یلدن زیاده راق امامتلیک لوازمنی ادا ایدب آننک وفاتی بعدنده ینکی مسجد بناسندن بو یاق شریک امام بولب تورغان ملّا حسام الدین ابن ملّا زین العبدین مستقل امام بولدی \\ برآز یلدن صونکره بو ذات معزول اولب شاکردلرندن بریسی ... امام نصب قیلندی \\ بو مسجدنک قربنده ینه قضاق طائفه سندن تلاوبای آبدان اوغلی بر مدرسه بنا قیلمش \\ بو مسجدنک اهالیسی ۸۰۰ = اوی مقداری دیورلر \12b\ بونک ایللی آلتمش اوی مقداری کوفیس مشچان غیریسی کلّاً قضاق طائفه سیدر \\ بو مسجدده بزم بلدکمز مؤذن اوستکامن امامی ملّا علی ننک آتاسی ولید اوزاق مدت مؤذن بولوب ۱۱۰ یاشنده وفات ایتمش ثانی ملّا عبدالله نامنده ذات مؤذن اولدی

۶نچی نومر مسجد

۱۸۲۹نچی یل مذکور جولامان مسجدنه متصل محله ده واق تنوبای بای کوکن اوغلی بر مسجد بنا قیلب بونکا ابتدا قزاقدن باباجان اسملی بر

ذات امام بولدی بعده اوفا اویازلیک نعمت‌جان نام ذات امام بولدی بوننک ایامنده مسجد ۶نچی نومر عددنه داخل بولدی \\ ثم ملّا احمدجان آلتی بای امام بولدی \\ بو محله ۱۵۰ اوی مقداری تماماً قضاقدر

۷نچی نومر مسجد

اهالی کوبایکان سری بر محله زیاده‌لنمک عادة اولدقدن جماعت اتفاقله آقچه جیوب ۱۸۵۲نچی یلده بر مسجد دخی بنا قیلدیلر \\ بونکا اوّل امام بخاراء شریفده تحصیل قیلغان مچکاره قریه سی ننک ملّا زین العابدین بن عبدالمنان امام بولدی \\ بو ذات بر نچه یلدن صونک فالج زحمتی ایله متبلا اولدقدن مؤذن مصطفی سعید اوغلی بش یل مقداری امامتلیک لوازمنی ادا ایدب توردی امامنک وفاتی بعدنده ۱۸۶۳نچی یل بخاراده تحصیل قیلغان اوفا اویازلیک چالپو قریه سنده ملّا فضل الله بن نعمة الله امام بولدی بو ذات سل مرضنه مبتلا اولدقدن شول یلده وفات قیلب اورننه دملّا احمد ولی بن علی اوطاری بخارادن قایتوب امام و هم آخوند بولدی \\ بو ذات هجریه ۱۳۱۸نچی ۱۹۰۱نچی یلده حج سفرینه چقب یولده ادیس بلده سنده وفات اولمغله اوغلی ملّا فضل الله اکرم جای نشین اب بولمشدر \\ بو مسجدده \13a\ مؤذن اوّل ثابت ملّا ۲نچی مصطفی مؤذن ۳نچی محمدجان مؤذن ابن مصطفی

۸نچی نومر مسجد

جماعت کوبایدکدن ینه بر محله لازم بولب ۱۸۵۹نچی یل‌لرده عتیت الله اسملی بای بر مسجد بنا قیلب بو مسجدکه قزان نواحی قاز قریه سندن ملّا حسام الدین نام ذات امام بولدی \\ بعده بخاراء شریفده

تحصیل و ختم کتب قیلغان مسلم آولندن ملّا عبدالجبار ابن عبیدالله مذکور حسام الدین که داماد و هم امام معین بولوب توردی ملّا حسام الدین نک وفاتی بعدنده مستقل امام و مدرس بولدی \\ ۱۸۸۱نچی یل هجریه ۱۲۹۹نچی سنه ده حج شریفه واریب قایتوشنده طورسیاده وفات بولمشدر رحمة الله علیه بعده بخاراء شریفدن اوغلی صلاح الدین قایتوب یتکانچه دملّا کمالالدین و ملّا مالک و بعده ملّا عبدالحق بر آز مدت لر امام بولب صلاح الدین قایتدقدن صونکره آتاسی اورننه امام بولمشدر \\ بو مسجدکه اوّل مؤذن صفی الله ۲نچی عبیدالله ۳نچی ...

\13b\ ۹نچی نومر مسجد

ینه جماعت کوبایوب مسجدکه یراقلق قیلغاندن کین ۱۸۸۲نچی یلی که هجرتننک ۱۳۰۰نچی سنه سی ایدی تاشکچو قریه سندن حاجی محمدجان بای اسماعیل اوغلی اشتراکوف بر کوزل مسجد بنا قیلدی \\ بونکا امام و مدرس دملّا کمال الدین ابن محمدرحیم امام نصب قیلندی \\ بو ذات ابتدا قشقارده اسماعیل حضرتدن تحصیل بعده بخاراء شریفده تکمیل علوم ایتمش ذاتدر \\ بو مسجده مؤذن عبیدالله دور ۸نچی نومر مسجدده صفی مؤذنکه معین منزله سنده تورمش ایدی

اوشبو منک اوچ یوز اوتوزنچی هجریه که ۱۹۱۲نچی میلادیه که قدر سیمی پالاتده مساجدلرنک توقزی مفتی نظاراتنده ایکسی که چاله قضاق مسجدی یاخود سرد مسجدی دیرلر صدر کلامده یازلمشدر بری مناره سز و بری قوش مناره لی دور \\ مجموع نفوسی موثوق الکلم آدملرنک خبری ایله اوشبو تاریخده اوتوز منک مقداری عدد اولوب خانه حسابی دورت منکه قریب وار دیورلر \\ ایکی چاست دور \\ روسیه مملکتنده قزان و رنبوردن صونکره مسلمان آباد شهرنک بری اولب اهالیسی ۱۳۰۰ سنه لر حدودنه قدر قدیمی اوضاعندن آیریلمیوب اوزبیک سماق بی تکلف

ایسه لرده مزبور تاریخدن بو یاق کوب اوزکاریش اولدیغنی سویلیورلر

توقال مسجد ابتدا بناسندن بو یاق تعمیر و تجدید ایدلمیوب چونکه
محله سنده دولتمند آدم اولمدقدن و همده مسجدنی تعمیر و تجدیدینه
حکومتدن اجازة درکار اولوب اگر اعلام ایدلسه اوّلده بی رخصت
صالندیغی سببدن منع ایدلمک \14a\ اندیشه سی دخی دار و خاطر اوله
رق ۱۳۲۸نچی هجریه یه قدر مجاله قالوب فنایه قریب اولمش ایکان
مذکور تاریخده میلادنک ۱۹۱۰نچی یل لریدر سیمی نک معتبر
اغنیاسندن حاجی علی افندی حاجی احمدی اوغلی حسینف کوزل تجدید
ایتدیکی مسموعمز اولدی \\ خدا احساننی مقبول ایلیه

یازلمش نومرلی مساجدلرنک هر برنده مکتب و مدرسه لری اولوب فقط
توقال مسجد ایله بوقاچ بای مسجدننک مدرسه سی یوقدر \\ مذکور
مدرسه لرده ۱۳۲۵نچی سنه لره قدر اصول قدیم ایله اوقولوب مزبور
تاریخده بر باغادیلنی و هم صالنوب و هم بعض مکتب لرده دخی اصول
جدید باشلنمش ایسه ده ۱۳۳۰نچی سنه ده تاش مسجد مدرسه سنده
اصول جدید اسمی قالدرلوب ایسکی طرزده اوقولمق مصلحت کورلمشدر

Bei Fragen zur Produktsicherheit wenden Sie sich bitte an:
If you have any questions regarding product safety,
please contact:

Walter de Gruyter GmbH
Genthiner Straße 13
10785 Berlin
productsafety@degruyterbrill.com